EDITION

A POWE ... EVERYONE

MY DAILY SOLUTIONS

+412 POWERFUL PRAYER POINTS

SEPTEMBER-DECEMBER

Vol 6: Sections 9, 10, 11, 12

Published by Restoration Publishing

Contributor: Antonina Nanjo

www.mydailysolutions.org
bishopnanjo@gmail.com
info@mydailysolutions.org

ISBN: 978-1-915802-55-2

My Daily Solutions Vol 6: 9-12

For Global Distribution and Christian Bookshops

WhatsApp: +447971343765

Email us to: info@mydailysolutions.org **Also visit:**
www.mydailysolutions.org

TABLE OF CONTENTS

FOUR MAJOR KEY STEPS TO MDS

1. **PRAY:** Start your daily devotion with a prayer of thanksgiving, confession of sins, and prayers of understanding from the Holy Spirit, who is our Teacher.
2. **READ:** Read the passage of the day carefully and prayerfully, to receive what God is saying to you.
3. **MEDITATE:** Give your whole soul and spirit to the reading of the day. Pay full attention to the passage without distractions. Observe the lessons and think about them verbally and mentally, in pictures of the mind.
4. **SHARE:** Sharing your daily response with others is a way of retaining the lessons learned in your spirit man. As you repeat what you know to others, it stays with you forever.

Bishop James Nanjo and MDS
team would like to hear from you

SCAN HERE

TO SEND YOUR PRAYER REQUESTS & TESTIMONIES

HOW TO USE MDS

1. Begin each day by preparation through prayer. Pray that the Holy Spirit will illuminate the eyes of your understanding.
2. Carefully read the Bible passages and the articles. Take time to meditate and absorb the issues for the day.
3. Respond to the lessons of the day for personal reflections and group discussions, if possible.
4. Use the daily prayers as a guide for maximum impact for solutions.
5. Use your lessons from the devotional to prayerfully set weekly and monthly targets for spiritual growth.
6. Use the powerful prayer points in this devotional for personal deliverance and success in life.
7. Share your testimonies of how God has been blessing your life through the devotional.
8. Try and follow the one-year Bible reading plan.
9. Keep a personal notebook to write lessons learned and things to do. My Daily Solutions Journal is available to help you record your insights and revelations.
10. When you are blessed, get more copies for your network of friends.
11. Climax your devotion by anointing yourself with anointing oil.

TAKE NOTE

PARTNER WITH BISHOP JAMES NANJO TODAY

The monthly world missions partners of bishop james nanjo are a global communion of believers, who are being used of god to aid our world missions agenda. We have touched over 45 nations of the world. Currently, our focus is on asia pacific, with a population of over 4.5 Billion people--over half of the world's population. Let god use you to join the army today!

All seeds should be sowed into the following accounts:

ACCOUNTS DETAILS

UK: WISE BANK: Sort Code: 231470 // Accounts Number: 91738664

GHANA: STANBIC BANK// Accounts Holder: James Nanjo// Accounts Number: 9040004417695

GHANA (MTN MOBILE MONEY): 0556729900

CASH UP: $JamesNanjo

PAYPAL: paypal.me/rccglobal

ZELLE: drnanjo@gmail.com

STOP HERE!
SAY THE PRAYER OF SALVATION TODAY

Dear friend, to understand and receive the best of this devotional, you must decide on receiving and accepting Jesus Christ as your Lord and personal Saviour. ***"For it is by believing in your heart that you are made right with God, and it is by openly declaring your faith that you are saved" (Romans 10:10; NLT).*** You must believe in your heart that Jesus is your Saviour and confess with your mouth that he is your Lord and personal Saviour.The best thing that will ever happen to you is to be born again.

PRAYER OF SALVATION

My Father God, I believe with all my heart that Jesus Christ your Son. I believe He died and rose again for my sake. I believe Jesus Christ is alive today and confess with my mouth that He is my Lord and Saviour from today and forever. Thank you, Father God, for eternal life. I am now a child of God. Praise God.

To grow your spiritual life after receiving Jesus Christ, you must look for a Bible-believing church where you will be fed with the unadulterated Word of God for spiritual growth. You can also get in touch with us through the contacts below:

Email: info@mydailysolutions.org
WhatsApp: +447971343765

PARTNER WITH US TODAY

MY DAILY SOLUTIONS GLOBAL PARTNERS

(MDSGP)

Our goal is to place this daily devotional in schools, universities, hospitals, homes, and all public places. Our target list includes nations, cities, towns, and even villages. Just imagine what will happen to the glory of God when you partner with us every month as MDSGP, to support our mandate of reaching multitudes with My Daily Solutions.

Below are ways you can become an MDSGP:

- You can partner with us to sponsor 30 copies or more, every quarter.
- You or your business can partner with us to adopt and sponsor a school, community, or city on monthly basis.
- You can partner with us by becoming a quarterly distributor of the devotional or you can become our covenant partner with a commitment of monthly donations that will help us communicate the good news of Jesus Christ in a city near you via TV, Radio, and Online.
- Your donation will also help our community initiative projects of building boreholes, helping orphans, and making donations to underprivileged communities.

Be a part of this special mission through your financial partnership with us to reach out and sponsor people in every city with the My Daily Solution message of Jesus Christ.

412 POWERFUL PRAYERS FOR SUCCESSFUL LIVING

POWERFUL DAYTIME PRAYERS FOR SUCCESSFUL LIVING

PRAYER FOR FINISHING WELL

1. O Lord, destroy every power stopping me from finishing well, in Jesus' name.
2. Father, give me grace and strength to finish my race with joy.
3. By Jesus' power, I receive supernatural momentum to finish strong.
4. Every barrier to my completion, collapse now by fire!
5. Lord, remove every obstacle and distraction from my path.
6. Powers planning my failure, scatter by the blood of Jesus!
7. I receive fresh anointing to stay focused and determined.
8. God of speed, help me recover lost ground and finish greater.
9. Holy Spirit, renew my vision and restore my steps.
10. Anoint me to see the fulfillment of every promise over my life.
11. I silence every voice of defeat; I will finish with honor.
12. Spirit of unfinished projects, lose your hold over my destiny.
13. Father, let my testimony be that I finished well, in Jesus' name.

PRAYER FOR PREGNANCY AND CONCEPTION

14. Father, bless me with the gift of conception and healthy pregnancy.
15. Lord, let my body be fruitful and ready to receive new life.
16. Remove every barrier to conception in my life, in Jesus' name.
17. Fill me with hope and patience as I wait for this miracle.
18. Protect my womb and prepare it for a safe and joyful pregnancy.
19. Strengthen my body and mind for this new season ahead.
20. Lord, grant my partner and me unity, peace, and love on this journey.
21. Silence every negative report and surround me with Your promises.
22. Guide me to caring doctors and supportive people along the way.
23. Let every stage of pregnancy be filled with peace and good health.
24. Cover my unborn child with Your protection and love.
25. Thank You, Lord, for the miracle of new life and answered prayer.

26. Father, let my testimony bring hope to others believing for their own miracle.

PRAYER TO CANCEL MISCARRIAGES

27. Father, I reject every form of miscarriage in Jesus' name.
28. My womb is a safe place; no power will terminate this pregnancy.
29. God's protection surrounds my unborn child, in Jesus' name.
30. Every plan of the enemy against my pregnancy is destroyed.
31. I decree my baby will live and not die, in Jesus' name.
32. Holy Spirit, fill this pregnancy with life and strength.
33. I silence fear and anxiety; I receive peace in Jesus' name.
34. Father, give my body strength to carry this child to full term.
35. I cancel every negative report and stand on God's promises.
36. Every curse or pattern of miscarriage is broken by Jesus' blood.
37. Lord, keep my baby strong and healthy by Your mighty hand.
38. My story will be of safe delivery and joy and no miscarriage, in Jesus' name.

PRAYER FOR ACADEMIC EXCELLENCE

39. Father, give me wisdom and understanding in all my studies.
40. Lord, open my mind to grasp every subject with ease.
41. I break every barrier holding back my academic progress.
42. Holy Spirit, guide me to excel in every exam and assignment.
43. I reject confusion and declare clarity of mind, in Jesus' name.
44. Father, grant me favor with my teachers and examiners.
45. I receive supernatural memory to recall everything I learn.
46. Every spirit of failure in my academics, be destroyed now.
47. I declare I will finish this academic season with excellence.
48. Lord, connect me with the right friends and mentors for success.
49. Father, let doors of scholarships and opportunities open for me.
50. My results will testify of God's faithfulness, academic success is my portion!

PRAYER FOR THE NATIONAL LEADERS

51. Father, grant our leaders wisdom to govern with justice and truth.
52. Lord, surround our leaders with good counsel and upright advisors.
53. I pray for leaders with integrity, compassion, and a heart for the people.

54. God, protect our leaders from every plan of evil and confusion.
55. Holy Spirit, inspire our leaders to make decisions that bring peace.
56. Father, help our leaders to walk in humility and serve selflessly.
57. Lord, raise up leaders who fear You and honor Your ways.
58. I pray for unity and understanding among those in authority.
59. God, remove every corrupt influence from our nation's leadership.
60. Father, let Your justice, righteousness, and blessing fill our land through wise leadership.

PRAYER FOR YOUR BIRTHDAY

61. I decree today that as I celebrate my birthday, it will mark the birth of many blessings in Jesus' mighty name.
62. My Father God of Abraham, place your seal of peace, fruitfulness, and mercy upon my life.
63. I receive grace on this covenant day of my life to live strong, long and young in Jesus' mighty name.
64. My Father God, I am forever grateful for your faithfulness in my life. Be glorified oh Lord.
65. God of Abraham, my future is in Your hands and I am grateful it will come with good news and joy.
66. My covenant Father in heaven, thank You for this special day of divine addition over my life.
67. My Father God, I ask that Your angelic envoys will continue to watch over me in my journey of long life.
68. Father God, I ask that in my new age, You will bless me with supernatural wisdom.
69. My covenant-keeping God, bless me continually with corresponding strength and ability in my new age.
70. Thank you Father God for bringing me into this world with a divine purpose. I am grateful for today.
71. My covenant-keeping God, lay Your hands of total prosperity upon my life in the name of Jesus Christ.

PRAYER FOR YOUR CHURCH

72. Lord, show us what spiritual milk is, and stir us away from falsehood.
73. Oh Lord, may our treasure be in You in our fellowship.
74. Remove worldly desires from the heart of Your church, that we may fully seek and pursue You.

75. Oh Lord, cause our hearts to rest on Your Holy Word at all times.
76. Father, in Your great love, give me//give us a true revelation of Jesus Christ.
77. May each one of us, including all new believers, have a veritable hunger for God.
78. Precious Father, give us a heart to obey Your commandments.
79. Oh Lord, may we become desperately hungry for Your Word.
80. May we crave to apply Your Word to our lives daily.
81. Oh Father God, increase our yearning for spiritual growth, that we may fully build our lives on You.
82. Father, let the fear of God overwhelm every man and woman in this church.

PRAYER FOR SUPERNATURAL ANOINTING

83. Father, anoint me afresh for every assignment before me.
84. Holy Spirit, let Your supernatural power rest upon my life.
85. I receive the anointing to do what I could never do by myself.
86. Lord, let Your anointing break every yoke in my life.
87. Fill me with boldness and spiritual authority, in Jesus' name.
88. Father, let Your presence flow through me to bless others.
89. I declare fresh oil for every new season and challenge.
90. Lord, make me a vessel of miracles, signs, and wonders.
91. By Your anointing, let every area of my life experience divine turnaround.
92. Father, set me apart by Your anointing for greatness.
93. Lord, let supernatural anointing distinguish me in my generation.

PRAYER FOR THE GREAT HARVEST OF SOULS

94. Father, give me a deep passion for the lost and hurting.
95. Lord, open doors for the gospel in my community and beyond.
96. Holy Spirit, prepare hearts everywhere for the message of Jesus.
97. Use me, Lord, as a vessel to bring many into Your kingdom.
98. I pray for boldness to share my faith with love and truth.
99. Father, let every word I speak draw people closer to Christ.
100. Remove every barrier that stops people from accepting Jesus.
101. Lord, let signs and wonders follow the preaching of Your word.
102. Soften even the hardest hearts to the saving power of the gospel.

103. Father, raise up more soul-winners in this generation.
104. I declare whole families, cities, and nations will turn to Jesus.
105. Lord, let there be a mighty revival and harvest in our time.
106. Holy Spirit, grant me compassion and wisdom in reaching the lost.
107. Father, let my life shine so others may see Christ and be saved.

PRAYER FOR TRAVELLING MERCIES

108. Father, I commit every journey I take into Your hands for safety.
109. Lord, protect me from accidents, harm, and danger as I travel.
110. Keep me and my loved ones safe on every road, flight, or route.
111. I pray for alertness and wisdom for every driver and pilot.
112. Lord, let Your angels go ahead of me and surround me on every side.
113. Remove every obstacle and keep delays and disruptions far from me.
114. Father, let every vehicle and means of transport work perfectly.
115. Bring me to my destination in peace and with a grateful heart.
116. I pray for calm weather and clear paths on every journey.
117. Thank You, Lord, for covering me with travelling mercies wherever I go.

PRAYER FOR FINANCIAL FLOW INTO BUSINESS

118. Father, open fresh doors of opportunity for my business today.
119. Lord, bless the work of my hands and multiply my efforts.
120. I receive wisdom to make sound financial decisions in my business.
121. Father, connect me with the right people and partners for success.
122. Let every financial barrier in my business be broken, in Jesus' name.
123. Lord, send divine helpers and clients to support and grow my business.
124. I declare steady cash flow and increased profit in my business.
125. Father, protect my business from loss, theft, and fraud.
126. Lord, give me creative ideas for growth and expansion.
127. Every plan of the enemy against my finances is cancelled.
128. Father, help me to honor You with my business and resources.
129. I receive favor in the marketplace and everywhere I go.
130. Lord, let my business be a blessing to others and my community.
131. Father, remove every delay to payment and breakthrough.
132. I thank You, Lord, for supernatural provision and open doors.
133. Lord, let my testimony be abundance, success, and overflow in my business.

MIDNIGHT PRAYERS OF DELIVERANCE FOR BREAKTHROUGHS

PRAYER TO CANCEL NIGHTMARES

134. Father, I cancel every nightmare and evil dream, in Jesus' name.
135. Lord, fill my sleep with Your peace and protection tonight.
136. I reject every spirit of fear, terror, or torment in my dreams.
137. Holy Spirit, guard my mind and heart as I rest.
138. Let every plan of the enemy against my sleep be destroyed.
139. I declare sweet, refreshing sleep over my life, in Jesus' name.
140. Father, remove every negative memory or image from my dreams.
141. Lord, surround my room and mind with Your angels as I sleep.
142. Father, let the blood of Jesus cover my thoughts and dreams.
143. I decree my nights will be filled with visions of hope and encouragement.
144. Lord, give me divine dreams and heavenly encounters as I sleep.

DELIVERANCE FROM DEMONIC RESTRICTIONS

145. Father, break every demonic chain holding me back, in Jesus' name.
146. Lord, destroy every invisible barrier set against my progress.
147. I reject every limitation placed on my life by the enemy.
148. Holy Spirit, set me free from every form of spiritual bondage.
149. I cancel every negative word and curse spoken over my destiny.
150. Every stronghold of darkness in my life, be shattered by God's power.
151. Father, release me from every cage of delay and frustration.
152. I declare total freedom from every evil pattern in my family line.
153. Lord, disconnect me from every unholy soul tie or evil covenant.
154. Every monitoring spirit following my life, be blinded and cast out.
155. I receive boldness and authority to walk in my God-given freedom.
156. Father, silence every accusing voice of the enemy against me.
157. Lord, let Your fire consume every demonic presence around me.
158. I decree open doors and unstoppable progress from today forward.
159. Thank You, Lord, for my deliverance and new freedom in Christ.

DELIVERANCE FROM WILDERNESS SPIRIT

160. Father, break every demonic chain holding me back, in Jesus' name.
161. Lord, destroy every invisible barrier set against my progress.

162. I reject every limitation placed on my life by the enemy.
163. Holy Spirit, set me free from every form of spiritual bondage.
164. I cancel every negative word and curse spoken over my destiny.
165. Every stronghold of darkness in my life, be shattered by God's power.
166. Father, release me from every cage of delay and frustration.
167. I declare total freedom from every evil pattern in my family line.
168. Lord, disconnect me from every unholy soul tie or evil covenant.
169. Every monitoring spirit following my life, be blinded and cast out.
170. I receive boldness and authority to walk in my God-given freedom.
171. Father, silence every accusing voice of the enemy against me.
172. Lord, let Your fire consume every demonic presence around me.
173. I decree open doors and unstoppable progress from today forward.
174. Thank You, Lord, for my deliverance and new freedom in Christ.

PRAYER TO CURE EVERY SICKNESS

175. Father, I ask for Your healing touch over every sickness in my body.
176. Lord, cure every hidden disease and restore my health completely.
177. By the stripes of Jesus, I declare total healing over my life.
178. Every pain and discomfort in my body, disappear in Jesus' name.
179. Holy Spirit, strengthen every weak area in my body and mind.
180. I reject every diagnosis of infirmity—I receive wholeness today.
181. Lord, heal me from the inside out and renew my strength daily.
182. Father, protect me from recurring illness and lingering symptoms.
183. Let every cell, organ, and system in my body align with divine health.
184. Thank You, Lord, for being my healer and restoring me to full health.

PRAYER FOR DESTINY HELPERS

185. Holy Spirit, connect me with my destiny helpers in the name of Jesus.
186. Fire of God, explode in my life to bring the right people, in the name of Jesus.
187. Every satanic veil covering me from my destiny helpers, be burnt by fire in the name of Jesus.
188. God of Abraham, cause the anointing for prosperity to fall upon me now, in the name of Jesus Christ.
189. Grace for divine connection, locate me now, in the name of Jesus Christ.

190. Every demonic authority fighting my destiny be destroyed now, in the name of Jesus Christ.
191. Lord, let the heavens open upon me now, in the name of Jesus Christ.
192. Every power, working against my prosperity by removing helpers, fall and perish, in the name of Jesus Christ.
193. Every power that wants to deny me of my destiny by removing helpers, catch fire, in the name of Jesus Christ.
194. I decree I will never lack help in this season.
195. Oh God of Abraham, let my helpers be willing to help me.
196. My Father God, deliver my helpers from wicked attacks.
197. Those that say wicked things about me to block help from my helpers, be exposed by fire by the Blood of Jesus.
198. I decree divine protection over my helpers and their helpers by the Blood of Jesus Christ.

JUDGMENT OVER HOME BREAKERS

199. Father, expose and judge every force trying to destroy my home.
200. Lord, scatter every plan of home breakers against my family.
201. I declare confusion in the camp of those sowing division in my household.
202. Every evil hand trying to tear my family apart, wither in Jesus' name.
203. Lord, restore unity and love wherever the enemy has sown discord.
204. Father, shield my marriage and home from every strange spirit or influence.
205. Let every hidden agenda to break my family be revealed and destroyed.
206. I plead the blood of Jesus over my home—no weapon formed against us shall prosper.
207. Thank You, Lord, for fighting for my family and keeping us together.

PRAYER FOR A BLISSFUL MARRIAGE

208. Father, let Your love fill my marriage every single day.
209. Lord, teach us to communicate with kindness, honesty, and patience.
210. Strengthen our bond and keep us united, even in tough seasons.
211. Help us to forgive quickly and always seek peace with each other.
212. Lord, bless our home with joy, laughter, and sweet companionship.
213. Remove every misunderstanding and replace it with understanding and grace.

214. May our marriage reflect Your love and be a light to others.
215. Protect us from outside influences that seek to divide us.
216. Give us wisdom to face challenges together and grow stronger.
217. Thank You, Lord, for making our marriage a source of blessing and bliss.

PRAYER FOR LONG LIFE

218. Father, thank You for the gift of life—let me live out my days in good health.
219. Lord, protect me from every danger and accident that shortens life.
220. I reject every spirit of premature death over me and my loved ones.
221. Strengthen my body, mind, and spirit for a long and purposeful life.
222. Keep me safe from sickness and disease, in Jesus' name.
223. Guide my steps daily so I will not walk into harm's way.
224. Lord, fill my years with joy, peace, and fulfillment.
225. Let me see my children's children and leave a godly legacy.
226. Satisfy me with long life and show me Your salvation.
227. Thank You, Lord, for promising me long, fruitful, and blessed years.

PRAYER BEFORE YOUR MARRIAGE CEREMONY

228. Father, thank You for bringing us to this special moment in our lives.
229. Lord, guide every step of our wedding preparations with Your wisdom.
230. Let Your presence fill our ceremony and bring us joy and peace.
231. Protect us from every plan of the enemy on our wedding day.
232. Bless our union and make it a testimony of Your faithfulness.
233. Provide for every need and let everything work together smoothly.
234. Surround us with love, support, and true friends on this journey.
235. Grant us calm hearts and minds as we step into this new season.
236. Let our marriage begin with Your blessing and favor resting on us.
237. Thank You, Lord, for making this day a beautiful beginning to our life together.

PRAYER BEFORE CHURCH GATHERING

238. Father, thank You for the privilege to gather as Your people today.
239. Lord, prepare our hearts and minds to receive from You.
240. Let Your Holy Spirit fill this place and guide every part of our meeting.

241. Cover everyone attending with Your protection and peace.
242. Let every distraction and spirit of confusion be removed from our midst.
243. Father, let Your presence bring healing, encouragement, and breakthrough today.
244. Bless everyone serving, musicians, ushers, teachers, and leaders.
245. Unite us in worship, love, and purpose as one family in Christ.
246. Let Your word come alive and speak directly to every heart.
247. May every burden be lifted and every need be met in Your presence.
248. Give us joy and freedom as we praise and honor You together.
249. Lord, let new friendships and connections be formed today.
250. Fill our gathering with miracles, testimonies, and Your undeniable power.
251. Thank You, Lord, for what You are about to do in our midst today.

PRAYER FOR ACADEMIC SUCCESS

252. My Father God, grant me focus and diligence in my studies.
253. Father God, remove distractions that hinder my academic success.
254. Father God, fill me with wisdom and understanding in my academic life.
255. Father God, help me retain and understand all I study for success.
256. Father God, grant me the desire and discipline for my studies.
257. Lord Jesus, help every struggling student see their potential by your help.
258. Father God, forgive me for neglecting my studies and grant me restoration.
259. Father God, override my fear of failure with Your mercy.
260. Father God, consume procrastination and laziness in my life.
261. Father God, reward my hard work with academic success.
262. Φather God, remove confusion and forgetfulness from my studies.
263. Father God, open doors of academic excellence for me.
264. Father God, give me peace over exams and assignments.
265. Father God, increase my joy and passion for learning.
266. I decree success in all my academic work.
267. I cancel failure and shame in all my exams and academic work.
268. I receive uncommon grace for academic excellence and breakthroughs.

PRAYER TO CONQUERING LIFE'S CHALLENGES

269. Father, help me to rise above every obstacle in my path.
270. Lord, give me clarity and wisdom when I face tough decisions.
271. Strengthen my faith when circumstances seem impossible.
272. Surround me with Your peace in the midst of every storm.
273. Let hope spring up in my heart, even when I feel discouraged.
274. Guide my words and actions so I reflect Your love under pressure.
275. Send me the right people and support when I need it most.
276. Lord, help me persevere and not lose heart during hard times.
277. Open my eyes to opportunities and solutions I might not see.
278. Father, heal the wounds that life's battles have left behind.
279. Give me resilience to keep moving forward, no matter what.
280. Let every challenge turn into a testimony of Your goodness.
281. Keep me grateful and trusting, even when things don't go my way.
282. Lord, fill my heart with joy and strength for each new day.
283. Thank You, Lord, for always carrying me through every challenge.

PRAYER TO CANCEL EVIL REPORT

284. I reject every evil report spoken over my life, in Jesus' name.
285. Lord, let only Your word and promises stand true for me.
286. Silence every voice of negativity and fear trying to shake my faith.
287. I cancel every diagnosis, accusation, or prediction not from God.
288. Cover me and my family with Your protection from bad news.
289. Turn every negative report into a testimony of Your power.
290. Fill my heart with peace, no matter what I hear from others.
291. Father, help me to trust Your goodness above every circumstance.
292. Let the truth of Your love and faithfulness cancel every lie.
293. Thank You, Lord, that Your report is the final word over my life.

PRAYER TO FIND A LIFE PARTNER

294. Father, guide me to the right person You have chosen for me.
295. Lord, prepare my heart to love and be loved in a healthy way.
296. Remove every distraction or counterfeit relationship from my path.
297. Help me to wait patiently and trust Your perfect timing.
298. Give me wisdom to recognize true love and godly character.
299. Lord, let my future partner also be seeking You with all their heart.

300. Protect me from heartbreak and lead me away from wrong choices.
301. Surround me with friends and mentors who will encourage me.
302. Fill me with confidence and peace as I wait for Your best.
303. Thank You, Lord, for the beautiful love story You are writing for me.

PRAYER UNLOCKING YOUR DESTINY

304. Father, reveal to me the purpose and path You've designed for my life.
305. Lord, open every door that leads me closer to my destiny.
306. Remove every obstacle standing in the way of my divine assignment.
307. Give me clarity and boldness to pursue what You've called me to do.
308. Surround me with people who will encourage and support my destiny.
309. Lord, silence every voice of doubt and limitation in my heart.
310. Release fresh ideas, inspiration, and opportunities for my future.
311. Protect my destiny from every plan of the enemy.
312. Father, let my gifts make room for me and bring me before great people.
313. Thank You, Lord, for guiding me into the fullness of my destiny.

PRAYER FOR DEEP UNDERSTANDING

314. Father, open my mind to truly understand Your word and Your ways.
315. Lord, give me insight and wisdom beyond my natural abilities.
316. Help me to see things from Your perspective, not just my own.
317. Remove confusion and grant me clarity in every situation.
318. Holy Spirit, teach me deep truths that transform my life.
319. Let my heart be sensitive to Your voice and direction.
320. Help me apply what I learn so I grow in wisdom and grace.
321. Lord, connect me with mentors and friends who help me understand more.
322. Thank You, Father, for giving me light and understanding in all things.

PRAYER TO RAISE SUCCESSFUL CHILDREN

323. Father, give my children wisdom and understanding in all they do.
324. Lord, help them discover and develop their unique gifts and talents.
325. Protect them from negative influences and wrong friendships.
326. Fill their hearts with confidence, kindness, and godly character.

327. Guide them to make good choices and pursue their dreams with courage.
328. Surround them with mentors and friends who inspire them to grow.
329. Bless the work of their hands and let them succeed in every season.
330. Keep their hearts close to You, no matter where life takes them.
331. Thank You, Father, for making my children a testimony of success and grace.

CONQUER DEPRESSION AND ANXIETY

332. Father, lift every heavy burden and fill my heart with Your peace.
333. Lord, drive out every trace of fear, worry, and anxiety from my mind.
334. Remind me daily that I am not alone—You are always with me.
335. Replace every dark thought with hope, joy, and fresh perspective.
336. Give me strength to reach out for help and receive support when I need it.
337. Help me to rest in Your promises, even when I don't understand.
338. Surround me with loving people who will encourage and uplift me.
339. Heal every wound that triggers sadness or panic in my heart.
340. Thank You, Lord, for the victory, freedom, and new peace You give me.

PRAYER TO BE RELEVANT IN ALL SEASONS

341. Father, help me to stay useful and valuable no matter the season of my life.
342. Lord, teach me how to adapt and grow as life changes around me.
343. Give me fresh ideas and wisdom to remain effective where I am planted.
344. Open my eyes to new opportunities, even in challenging times.
345. Help me to keep learning and never become stagnant or stuck.
346. Let my gifts and abilities bless others in every stage of life.
347. Father, guide me to meet the real needs of people around me.
348. Keep my heart humble and open to change and new assignments.
349. Strengthen me to remain faithful and fruitful, whatever comes my way.
350. Lord, connect me with those who need what I have to offer.
351. Thank You, Father, for making me a blessing and keeping me relevant always.

PRAYER FOR A HIGHER DIMENSION

352. Father, take me deeper in my relationship with You this season.
353. Lord, open my eyes to see beyond the ordinary and step into new realms.
354. Give me fresh hunger for Your word and Your presence every day.
355. Stretch my faith to believe You for greater things in my life.
356. Pour out new anointing and spiritual gifts upon me, Lord.
357. Help me to leave my comfort zone and embrace Your higher calling.
358. Surround me with people who inspire me to grow higher in You.
359. Reveal mysteries and deeper truths to me through Your Spirit.
360. Let my life reflect Your glory and impact my world at new levels.
361. Thank You, Father, for lifting me into greater dimensions of purpose and power.

PRAYER FOR NEXT LEVEL PROSPERITY

362. Father, position me for uncommon opportunities and breakthroughs.
363. Lord, let doors of next-level prosperity open for me this season.
364. Give me divine connections that advance my purpose and resources.
365. Remove every limitation hindering my financial growth.
366. Pour out new streams of income and abundance into my life.
367. Let favor surround me and my work everywhere I go.
368. Teach me to manage blessings wisely as You increase me.
369. Protect me from every trap or scheme that leads to loss.
370. Give me boldness to step into higher levels of success.
371. May my prosperity create opportunities for others to be blessed.
372. Let every good thing I touch prosper and multiply.
373. Show me where to sow and invest for generational wealth.
374. Remove fear and help me trust You for more than enough.
375. Thank You, Lord, for taking me higher and making prosperity my reality.

PRAYER FOR GOD TO SEND GOOD PEOPLE INTO YOUR LIFE

376. Father, surround me with people who genuinely care about my growth.
377. Lord, connect me with friends who inspire and encourage me.
378. Remove every negative influence and wrong relationship from my life.
379. Bring mentors and wise counselors to guide my steps.
380. Send supportive people who help me fulfill my purpose.

381. Let my relationships be filled with honesty, trust, and understanding.
382. Help me to recognize and appreciate the good people You send my way.
383. Protect me from betrayal and disappointment in my friendships.
384. Bless me with loyal companions for every season of life.
385. Thank You, Father, for surrounding me with loving, uplifting people.

HOLY SPIRIT, USE ME

386. Holy Spirit, lead me to people who need Your touch today.
387. Give me sensitivity to recognize divine opportunities to serve.
388. Fill my heart with compassion for the hurting and lost.
389. Let Your wisdom flow through me in every conversation.
390. Use my hands to heal, bless, and comfort those around me.
391. Open my eyes to needs I might otherwise miss.
392. Give me courage to step out in faith when You prompt me.
393. Help me put others before myself, following Jesus' example.
394. Let my life radiate Your love, even in small, unseen ways.
395. Guide me in prayer for others who are struggling or searching.
396. Holy Spirit, use my talents and gifts to build Your kingdom.
397. Help me to speak words that lift, strengthen, and encourage.
398. Remove selfishness so I can serve with a pure heart.
399. Let every day be an opportunity to shine Your light.
400. Direct my steps and make me available for Your assignments.
401. Empower me to forgive quickly and love deeply.
402. Thank You, Holy Spirit, for using me to make a difference in the world.

PRAYING INTO A NEW YEAR

403. Father, thank You for Your faithfulness throughout the past year.
404. Lord, I dedicate this new year into Your loving hands.
405. Fill my days with purpose, joy, and new opportunities.
406. Help me to let go of disappointments and move forward in hope.
407. Guide my decisions so I stay on the path You have for me.
408. Surround me and my loved ones with Your protection and favor.
409. Open doors that no one can shut and close every wrong door.
410. Bless the work of my hands and bring increase this year.
411. Keep my heart grateful, humble, and full of faith in every season.
412. Thank You, Lord, for a year of answered prayers and new testimonies.

USE THIS DEVOTIONAL WITH MY DAILY SOLUTIONS JOURNAL

SEPTEMBER

WELCOME TO THE MONTH OF KINGSHIP

PROPHETIC DECREE

I decree that this month marks your divine reclassification, every inferior label and limitation is broken now. By the authority of Christ, I declare you are not lower, middle, or upper class, you are of the Jesus class, royalty, born to reign and serve with purpose and vision. This month, you will rediscover your true identity in Christ; the survival mindset will leave you, and you will think generationally, act sacrificially, and walk in kingly authority. Each day, the Holy Spirit will unveil new dimensions of your kingship. You are not who society says you are you are who God says you are: chosen, elevated, and empowered to lead with Christlike love. Walk boldly in your kingship. Welcome to your royal season.

KINGSHIP

Welcome to a new month, and welcome to a new mindset. This month's devotional is not just another 30 day reading plan. It is a prophetic invitation to rediscover your true identity in Christ. For many of us, growing up meant learning about society's class system: the lower class, the middle class, and the upper class. We were taught to measure ourselves by income brackets, education levels, or family background. But heaven has a different classification: one that overrides every earthly label.

If you are born of God, you are not lower class. You are not middle class. And even being upper class is far beneath your divine placement. You have been reclassified into the Jesus class. And because Jesus is King, you too are a king. That is not religious hype; it is scriptural truth. You were born into royalty the moment you were born again.

This month, each devotional entry will explore a different dimension of your kingship. You will learn what it means to carry royal traits. You will be challenged to reject the survival mindset, embrace purpose, think generationally, and live sacrificially. More importantly, you will see that kingship in God's kingdom is not about dominance; it is about service, vision, and Christlikeness.

As always, each day's entry is followed by three personal response questions and one prayer point. Do not rush them. Meditate. Reflect. Pray. Let the Spirit of God engrave these truths into your heart.

You are not who the world says you are. You are who God says you are: a king in the class of Christ.

Welcome home. Welcome to Kingship.

TABLE OF CONTENTS

BORN AGAIN INTO A KINGDOM

"Jesus answered and said unto him, Verily, verily, I say unto thee, Except a man be born again, he cannot see the kingdom of God.'" John 3:3

John 3:3 is more than a Bible verse; it is a royal announcement. It tells us plainly that being born again is the entry point into God's kingdom. It is not merely an emotional moment during a church altar call. It is not a religious ritual or the start of a moral lifestyle. It is your official induction into the dynasty of kingship. The moment you received Christ, you stepped out of the realm of mere religion and into the rule and reign of the King of kings.

Sadly, many believers do not act like they have entered a kingdom. They come into salvation but still carry the look of defeat, the posture of pain, and the attitude of victims. It is as though something is always dragging them backward. They walk around looking like life has beaten them beyond repair. That should not be your story. That is not the Christianity Jesus died to give us.

Let me say this as clearly as I can: that burden-laden brand of Christianity must cease. The idea that being born again is a pathway into constant suffering, depression, fear, and confusion is a lie from the pit of hell. You are not born again to struggle. You are born again into access. You have divine access that outpaces the internet, AI, WiFi, or any human system. The moment you became born again, your access to divine resources and heavenly authority was activated.

You are not born again into trial and error. You are not born again into darkness, sickness, or confusion. You are not born again into endless cycles of defeat. You are born again into joy. You are born again into peace. You are born again into laughter and deliverance. And most importantly, you are born again into kingship.

Quote of the Day: The idea that being born again is a pathway into constant suffering, depression, fear, and confusion is a lie from the pit of hell. You are not born again to struggle. You are born again into access.

PERSONAL RESPONSE:

1. Are you truly living with the awareness that you have been born again into a kingdom?
2. In what areas of your life are you still thinking or behaving like a victim instead of a child of the King?
3. How can you begin to walk in the joy, peace, and access that comes with your new birth in Christ?

Daily Prayer: Dear Lord, open my eyes to the reality of my new birth. Help me to stop thinking like a victim and start living like a citizen of Your kingdom. Let me walk in the access, authority, and joy that are mine in Christ, in Jesus' name, amen.

Read the Bible in One Year: 1 Chronicles 16-18

SEPTEMBER 02

A CALL TO CHANGE THE SCRIPT

"And be not conformed to this world: but be ye transformed by the renewing of your mind, that ye may prove what is that good, and acceptable, and perfect, will of God." Romans 12:2

Too many believers are living by a faulty script: one written by rejection, trauma, culture, and past experiences. They love God. They serve sincerely. Yet they live like paupers in a palace, children of the King, but operating like slaves. Something is not adding up. It is time to change the script.

You can be passionate about God and still trapped in a wrong mindset. You may shout "Amen" in church but still carry the lie that you are not enough. That is the tragedy, it is not salvation you lack, but revelation. Somewhere along the line, you picked up a script God never wrote. A script that says you are still a victim, still broken, still unwanted. Satan does not need to steal your salvation to keep you defeated. He just needs to cloud your identity. Trials, delays, and disappointments are his tools to distract you from who you really are. If you focus more on your struggle than your status in Christ, you will forfeit your crown without realizing it. But hear this: your identity is not defined by your battles. It is defined by Christ. You are not what you have been through; you are who God says you are, chosen, royal, His own. Heaven does not call you weak. Heaven calls you a king. Tear up the old script. Reject the lie that says you are unworthy. Embrace the truth that in Christ, you are more than a conqueror. You are not just a churchgoer; you are a Kingdom citizen. And in this Kingdom, you reign. The script has changed. Now it is time for you to live like it!

Quote of the Day: Your identity is not defined by your battles. It is defined by Christ.

PERSONAL RESPONSE:

4. What old script have you been living by that contradicts what God says about you?
5. In what areas of your life are you still thinking like a victim rather than a victorious child of the King?
6. How can you begin to renew your mind daily so you live according to your true identity in Christ?

Daily Prayer: Dear Lord, open my eyes to the false scripts I have believed. Help me to tear them up and fully embrace the truth of who I am in You. I choose to live as royalty, not as a victim. Transform me by the renewing of my mind, in Jesus' name, amen.

Read the Bible in One Year: 1 Chronicles 19-21; John 8

KINGS GATHER BEFORE THE KING OF KINGS

"He was king in Jeshurun, when the heads of the people were gathered, all the tribes of Israel together." Deuteronomy 33:5

There is a mystery in this verse: God is revealed not just as King, but as King in the midst of gathered kings. The "heads of the people" refers to tribal leaders, royalty in their own right. When they gathered, God manifested as their King. It was not just a religious meeting; it was a royal convocation.

This is the Kingdom pattern, the King of kings meets with kings. Church is not just a crowd of worshippers; it is a council of royalty. Every gathering is a royal summons. We do not come merely for songs and sermons; we come to align with the Ruler of heaven and earth.

Church is not a pit stop for the weary; it is a throne room for the regal. It is where kings receive strategy, strength, and spiritual alignment. That is why church services are sacred. When we assemble, God shows up not just as Father or Friend, but as King.

From verse 6 onward, Moses begins to declare blessings over each tribe. Why? Because when kings gather, blessings follow. Declarations are made, inheritances released, destinies activated.

If you see yourself as a mere attendee, you may miss it. But if you recognize yourself as part of heaven's royal assembly, you will come expecting divine encounters. Kingship without blessing is empty. A crown without content is powerless. Do not be a king in name but disconnected from divine empowerment.

Every church gathering is a throne invitation. Come as a king. Meet the King. And leave with your portion.

Quote of the Day: Church is not just a crowd of worshippers; it is a council of royalty. Every gathering is a royal summons. We do not come merely for songs and sermons; we come to align with the Ruler of heaven and earth.

PERSONAL RESPONSE:

1. When you attend church, do you see yourself as a passive participant or as a king answering a royal summons?
2. In what ways have you underestimated the spiritual weight and significance of gathering with other believers?
3. Are you positioning your heart to receive divine strategy, blessing, and alignment whenever you gather before the King?

Daily Prayer: Dear Lord, help me to never treat church gatherings lightly. Let me always come with expectation, honour Your presence as my King, and receive the divine portion You have prepared for me, in Jesus' name, amen.

Read the Bible in One Year: 1 Chronicles 22-24

SEPTEMBER 04

THE POWER OF THE BLESSING

"Gather yourselves together, that I may tell you that which shall befall you in the last days." Genesis 49:1

Genesis 49 gives us a prophetic moment: Jacob, near death, gathers his twelve sons,not to say goodbye, but to release destiny-shaping blessings. Each son receives a unique word, tailor-made for their identity and future. Judah is marked for kingship, Zebulun for the seas, Issachar for servanthood. This is the power of the blessing: it defines, unlocks, and empowers.

Jacob was not offering advice; he was legislating in the spirit. His words governed generations. That is the weight of a blessing: it activates kingship. Without it, your reign lacks authority. You may be a king by calling, but the blessing is what puts that calling into motion. It is God's endorsement on your assignment. Without it, kings walk like servants.

This principle did not begin with Jacob. It started in Eden. When God created Adam, He did not just place him in the garden; He blessed him:

"Be fruitful, and multiply... subdue it: and have dominion." Genesis 1:28

That blessing was not poetic; it was empowering. Adam operated with supernatural wisdom and authority. That is what kingship looks like: blessing-fuelled dominion.

Kingship is not about wearing a crow; it is about walking in divine purpose with heaven's backing. If you are born again, you are already a king. But without the blessing, your potential stays dormant. Many believers live in frustration, not from lack of identity, but lack of activation. So, value the blessing. Seek it. Speak it. Declare it. The power of the blessing is the fuel of your kingship.

Quote of the Day: You may be a king by calling, but the blessing is what puts that calling into motion. It is God's endorsement on your assignment. Without it, kings walk like servants.

PERSONAL RESPONSE:

1. Are you living with the awareness that your kingship in Christ needs the blessing to be activated and effective?
2. In what areas of your life have you embraced your identity but neglected to seek God's blessing for empowerment?
3. How intentional are you about speaking and declaring God's blessing over your life, family, and assignment?

Daily Prayer: Lord, I refuse to walk beneath my design. Activate every dimension of Your blessing in my life. Empower me to reign with wisdom, authority, and purpose, just as You intended, in Jesus' name, amen.

Read the Bible in One Year: 1 Chronicles 25-27

KINGS OPERATE IN A DIFFERENT CLASS

"And hath made us kings and priests unto God and his Father; to him be glory and dominion for ever and ever. Amen." Revelation 1:6

Your kingship in Christ is not symbolic; it is powerful and positional. The moment you were born again, you did not just join a church; you stepped into a kingdom. You became part of a royal lineage, lifted far above worldly systems and limitations. You are not ordinary. You were born to rule.

Look at Adam in the garden. He did not hustle; he spoke. God brought every creature to him, and whatever Adam called them, that became their name (Genesis 2:19). That was dominion in action. Adam was not waiting on heaven; he was acting on heaven's authority. That is kingly living.

As a believer, you have been raised with Christ and seated in heavenly places (Ephesians 2:6). You do not live under circumstances; you live above them. You function from the realm of insight, access, and dominion.

Sadly, many Christians live like victims: panicking, hustling, and thinking like those with no inheritance. That is not your class. This is not arrogance; it is revelation. You are from above.

Royalty does not run on sweat; it runs on grace. Grace gives you what effort cannot buy. It empowers you to work with wisdom, speak with authority, and walk in rest, even in chaos. Grace does not cancel responsibility; it amplifies effectiveness. It positions you to do in one year what others cannot do in ten.

Kings do not adjust downward to fit broken systems; they lead from above to change them. Kings do not follow fear; they move in faith. Kings do not bow to limits; they break them. So stop shrinking to fit in. You were not designed to blend; you were born to reign.

Quote of the Day: You were not designed to blend; you were born to reign.

PERSONAL RESPONSE:

1. Do you truly see yourself as a king in Christ, or have you been living like a victim of your circumstances?
2. In what areas of your life are you still operating by sweat instead of relying on grace?
3. How can you begin to lead from above rather than conforming to the broken systems around you?

Daily Prayer: Dear Lord, awaken me to the reality of my kingship in Christ. Help me to stop shrinking to fit in and start reigning by grace, authority, and divine wisdom in every area of my life, in Jesus' name, amen.

Read the Bible in One Year: 1 Chronicles 28-29; John 9

MAXIMIZE YOUR KINGSHIP IDENTITY

"For if by the one man's offense death reigned through the one, much more those who receive abundance of grace and of the gift of righteousness will reign in life through the One, Jesus Christ." Romans 5:17 (NKJV)

Are you truly living like someone who belongs to the King of kings? Or are you still waiting for permission to rise? It is tragic when a believer with divine authority lives like a beggar: settling, shrinking, and struggling. But kings do not beg. Kings do not live beneath their calling.

Romans 5:17 declares, *"…those who receive abundance of grace and of the gift of righteousness will reign in life through… Jesus Christ."* This is your assignment: to reign, not just survive. The world is not meant to define your life. You are called to shape the world around you.

Your situation does not redefine your identity. Even in adversity, your kingship stands. Kingship is not ease; it is authority. It means commanding peace in chaos and calling forth solutions where others see problems.

Stop living average when you carry supernatural authority. Your kingship gives you the right to speak, to build, to rule, and to restore. Do not wait for others. Step up and take your place. The world is waiting for the manifestation of kings.

This is not theory; it is a lifestyle that works. Kingship is not for show; it is for dominion. It is for changing narratives in families, businesses, and generations. No one can live this truth for you. If you do not embrace your royal identity, you will live like a servant in a palace. You will pray like a beggar when you were born to command. The power is there, but nothing happens until you activate it.

So put on your crown. Think like a king. Speak like a king. Move like a king. You are not becoming royalty; you already are.

Quote of the Day: The world is not meant to define your life. You are called to shape the world around you.

PERSONAL RESPONSE:

1. Are you walking daily in the authority and dominion that your identity in Christ provides, or are you still waiting for permission to rise?
2. In what areas of your life have you allowed your situation to redefine your identity instead of standing in your kingship?
3. What practical steps can you take this week to activate and walk boldly in your divine authority as a king in Christ?

Daily Prayer: Dear Lord, open my eyes to fully grasp my identity in You. Help me to stop living beneath my calling and to boldly walk in the authority, grace, and dominion You have given me as a king in Christ. In Jesus' name I pray, amen.

Read the Bible in One Year: 2 Chronicles 1-3; John 10

THE COMMUNITY OF KINGS

"But you are a chosen generation, a royal priesthood, a holy nation, His own special people, that you may proclaim the praises of Him who called you out of darkness into His marvellous light." 1 Peter 2:9

Imagine a people who know they have been chosen for greatness and set apart by God for something extraordinary. This is the Community of Kings: a royal priesthood, a holy nation, God's own special people. Their lives reflect the royal identity declared in 1 Peter 2:9.

The Church is not just a weekly gathering; it is heaven's embassy on earth. As citizens of this kingdom, we are called to reign in life, not alone but as a community. Together, we fulfil purpose, build each other up, and manifest God's kingdom. This community nurtures royal identity. It equips us to rule with authority, live with purpose, and walk in truth. Here, peace governs our hearts and relationships. Fruitfulness defines our families, careers, and ministries. Innovation flows freely, and creativity thrives, because we serve a limitless God.

We are not a people merely surviving; we are expanding, growing, and advancing. This is where light shines in darkness, where truth prevails, and where God's presence is tangible. At the heart of the Community of Kings is selfless, sacrificial, and Christlike love. It binds us, empowers service, and fuels our royal calling. This love is not just felt; it is lived. It is also a place of abundance: spiritually, emotionally, materially, and relationally. Testimonies of breakthrough and God's faithfulness abound. These are not just stories; they are living proof that the King is at work among His people. In the Community of Kings, individuals rise, and the whole community flourishes. This is where royalty is not just affirmed but also activated for the transformation of the world around us. You are royalty. And this is your community: the church of the living God!

Quote of the Day: As citizens of this kingdom, we are called to reign in life, not alone but as a community.

PERSONAL RESPONSE

1. Are you living daily with the mindset that you are part of a royal priesthood and a chosen community, or have you allowed culture and circumstances to define your identity?
2. How are you contributing to the strength, growth, and flourishing of your local "Community of Kings"?
3. In what ways can you reflect Christ-like love, fruitfulness, and kingdom values more intentionally within your church, workplace, or family?

Daily Prayer: Heavenly Father, open my eyes to fully embrace my royal identity in Christ. Help me to live purposefully within Your chosen community, reflecting Your love, walking in Your abundance, and advancing Your kingdom in every sphere of my life, in Jesus' name, amen.

Read the Bible in One Year: 2 Chronicles 4-6

SEPTEMBER 08

WHAT HAPPENS WHEN YOU FAIL TO MAXIMIZE COMMUNITY

"A man who isolates himself seeks his own desire; He rages against all wise judgment." Proverbs 18:1 (NKJV)

Remember Samson? Anointed, empowered, and destined to deliver Israel, yet his story ended in tragedy. Why? Because he walked alone. Though born into a covenant community, Samson lived in isolation. No counsel. No accountability. No kingdom friends. His failure was not a power failure; it was a community failure. Samson disregarded his vow, ignored wise counsel, and aligned with the wrong people. His eyes were gouged out, and his strength left him, not because God abandoned him, but because he abandoned the pattern. He chose isolation, and it devoured his destiny. Many believers today are repeating Samson's mistake: present but not planted. Surrounded by kings, yet disconnected. Attending services, posting scriptures, but emotionally low, stagnant, and unfruitful. No real integration. No covenant friendships. Just survival. Here is the truth: being near greatness does not benefit you unless you draw from it. God placed you in a royal community, not to observe, but to thrive. Every relationship in the Community of Kings carries purpose. If you do not discern it, you will waste it. Your next breakthrough may not come from a prayer but from a conversation, a divine connection, or a kingdom partnership. Wasted connections are equal to wasted years. Every delayed mentorship, ignored relationship, or withheld fellowship robs you of momentum. You are not the only king in the kingdom. God has placed other kings around you and you need them as much as they need you. You bring something they lack, and they carry something you need. Maximizing community means showing up, speaking up, and opening up. God is building more than your personal life. He is forming a royal house. Do not let pride, fear, or apathy keep you isolated. Connect. Engage. Align. Your greatness depends on it.

Quote of the Day: You are not the only king in the kingdom. God has placed other kings around you and you need them as much as they need you. You bring something they lack, and they carry something you need.

PERSONAL RESPONSE:

1. Have you been intentionally building meaningful, kingdom-aligned relationships within your church or community, or have you settled into quiet isolation?
2. Who are the people God has placed around you for your growth and accountability; and how have you honoured or ignored those connections?
3. Are there areas of your life where you have been struggling alone, instead of drawing strength from the Community of Kings God has planted you in?

Daily Prayer: Heavenly Father, I repent for every way I have isolated myself and neglected the kingdom relationships You have placed in my life. Help me to recognize, honour, and engage with my royal community. In Jesus' name, I pray. Amen.

Read the Bible in One Year: 2 Chronicles 7-9

HOW THE COMMUNITY OF KINGS FUNCTIONS

"The eye cannot say unto the hand, I have no need of thee: nor again the head to the feet, I have no need of you." 1 Corinthians 12:21

The Community of Kings is not just a gathering; it is a divine network where supply meets demand. No one carries everything, but everyone carries something. What you lack, someone else carries. God designed it that way. He hides answers in others to draw us into connection.

In 1 Corinthians 12:21, Paul reminds us, *"The eye cannot say to the hand, I have no need of you."* You are not meant to walk alone. Kings thrive best among kings.

Consider Moses. God gave him the vision for the tabernacle but not the skills to build it. That was Bezaleel's anointing. God also raised Aholiab and others to execute what Moses could only instruct. The pattern is clear: vision may rest on one, but fulfilment is distributed across many.

Everything you need (wisdom, counsel, provision) is within reach through divine connections. That project you are stuck on? Someone in your circle holds the key. That burden you carry? Another king has strength to lift it. But you must engage. Even Jesus did not walk alone. He had twelve. Among them, three. Isolation is not spirituality; it is sabotage.

Beware of pride and false humility. Do not suffer in silence. Do not pretend to have it all. God placed you in community for supply, sharpening, and success. When you withhold your need, you delay your breakthrough. So, ask. Offer. Honour. Receive. You are part of something bigger than yourself. Engage fully. Because the kingdom only advances when every joint supplies.

Quote of the Day: Isolation is not spirituality; it is sabotage.

PERSONAL RESPONSE

1. Where in your life are you trying to function alone, even though God has placed others around you to help?
2. Have you truly honoured the gifts, wisdom, and graces in the lives of other believers around you or have you been dismissive, envious, or disconnected?
3. What practical steps can you take this week to engage more deeply with your kingdom community?

Daily Prayer: Dear Lord, thank You for placing me in a royal community. I repent for every way I have ignored, isolated, or underestimated the people You sent to bless me. Open my eyes to the supply around me, and give me the humility to ask, the honour to receive, and the boldness to contribute. Help me to thrive through connection, not just survive in isolation. In Jesus' name, Amen.

Read the Bible in One Year: 2 Chronicles 10-12; John 11

SEPTEMBER 10

MAXIMIZING YOUR ROYAL COMMUNITY

"Iron sharpeneth iron; so a man sharpeneth the countenance of his friend." Proverbs 27:17

You were never meant to do life alone. God placed you in a royal community:, a kingdom ecosystem where every burden has a support, every need a supply.

Too many believers wrestle in silence while surrounded by people who carry what they need. Your community holds wisdom, grace, insight, and strength. But you must be planted. You must engage. Proverbs 11:14 says, *"Where no counsel is, the people fall: but in the multitude of counsellors there is safety."* Proverbs 27:17 adds, *"Iron sharpeneth iron..."* This is how royalty stays sharp: through connection, correction, and counsel.

Even Jesus said, *"Where two or three are gathered in My name, I am there..."* (Matthew 18:20). Kings sit at tables where other kings gather. That is where wisdom flows and blind spots are exposed. Isolation invites defeat. Connection produces strength. But you are not just a receiver; you are a distributor. You carry light, wisdom, and grace for others. Kings do not hoard; they pour. Someone is waiting for your encouragement, your insight, your presence. Think of Daniel and his three friends. Together, they transformed Babylon. They rose through unity, prayer, and excellence. Or David and his mighty men: bold warriors who fought with him and helped secure his throne. Their connection made victory possible. You, too, have warriors around you, intercessors, encouragers, helpers. Do not overlook them. Ask yourself: Who am I ignoring? Who should I be speaking to? Who am I sent to lift? Maximise your royal community. Show up. Speak up. Serve. Receive. Release. This is how kings rise together.

Quote of the Day: Isolation invites defeat. Connection produces strength.

PERSONAL RESPONSE

1. Who has God placed around you that you may have been overlooking or avoiding?
2. What gift or grace do you carry that you have not been sharing with your royal community?
3. Have you truly been planted and engaged in your kingdom circle or are you just present but disconnected?

Daily Prayer: Father, thank You for placing me in a royal community. Open my eyes to see the divine connections You have surrounded me with. Help me to walk in humility, serve with love, receive with grace, and contribute with boldness. Let every relationship ordained by You become fruitful for Your glory. In Jesus' name, Amen.

Read the Bible in One Year: 2 Chronicles 13-14

THE SKILL EVERY KING MUST HAVE

"Wisdom is the principal thing; therefore get wisdom: and with all thy getting get understanding." Proverbs 4:7

There is one skill every king in God's kingdom must develop: understanding. It is not optional. It is the defining trait that separates those who merely occupy spiritual positions from those who truly reign.

Understanding gives depth to knowledge, direction to wisdom, and power to potential. Without it, even the most gifted believers remain ineffective and misled. You may quote Scripture fluently, but if you do not understand its meaning or application, you are vulnerable. Understanding is what turns information into revelation, and revelation is what empowers victory. Proverbs 4:7 declares: *"Wisdom is the principal thing; therefore get wisdom: and with all thy getting get understanding."* That is not a suggestion; it is a divine command. Understanding is how you interpret times, manage resources, navigate seasons, and obey divine instructions with accuracy. You cannot substitute understanding with zeal or hide its absence behind religious activity. No amount of fasting can make up for it. Confusion is not always from the devil. Sometimes, it is the fruit of an untrained mind. You are not permitted to reign until you are trained; and you are not truly trained until you have been schooled in understanding. Life's battles often reveal what you do not understand. But when you gain insight, what once crippled others becomes your stepping stone. The difference between progress and stagnation, relevance and obscurity, victory and defeat is often just understanding. Where there is understanding, people become outstanding. Paths become clear. Strength is multiplied. Accuracy is restored. That is why every king must go deep. Understanding is the irreplaceable skill that separates kings from commoners.

Quote of the Day: Where there is understanding, people become outstanding, paths become clear, strength is multiplied and accuracy is restored. That is why every king must go deep.

PERSONAL RESPONSE:

1. Do you truly understand the truths you have received, or are you simply repeating what you have been taught?
2. How have you allowed a lack of understanding to delay your progress or complicate your decisions?
3. What intentional steps will you take this season to deepen your understanding in the areas where you have been confused or stagnant?

Daily Prayer: Dear Lord, I ask for a spirit of understanding. Deliver me from shallow thinking and surface living. Open my eyes to see, my ears to hear, and my heart to perceive what You are saying in this season. Train me to reign by giving me clarity, insight, and depth. In Jesus' name, Amen.

Read the Bible in One Year: 2 Chronicles 15-16; John 12

SEPTEMBER 12

A REQUEST THAT PLEASED GOD

"Give therefore thy servant an understanding heart to judge thy people, that I may discern between good and bad: for who is able to judge this thy so great a people?" 1 Kings 3:9

One of the most defining moments in King Solomon's life came when God gave him a blank cheque in 1 Kings 3. Solomon could have asked for power, wealth, or the death of his enemies, but he did not. His request was simple: *"Give therefore thy servant an understanding heart... "*

This one request revealed Solomon's depth. He knew that leadership without understanding would be disastrous. And God was pleased (see 1 Kings 3:11–12). God granted him understanding and added riches, honour, and long life. That is the principle: understanding unlocks everything else.

Too often, people chase wealth, favour, or promotion, while neglecting the key that unlocks them all. They receive dreams, words, and instructions, but without understanding, nothing changes. A word you do not understand cannot bless you.

Understanding is not a luxury; it is a necessity. It is what separates kings from amateurs. Many start ministries, marriages, businesses, and relationships without understanding their weight, and they crash under pressure they were not prepared for.

Solomon's request must become your posture: "Lord, give me understanding." Before you act, invest, or speak, seek understanding. Kings live by insight, not impulse. Emotion may be loud, but only understanding has depth.

So pause, Are you chasing results without insight? Are you acting without clarity? Understanding is still the request that pleases God, and it is the one that positions you to reign well.

Quote of the Day: Kings live by insight, not impulse. Emotion may be loud, but only understanding has depth.

PERSONAL RESPONSE:

1. Are you more focused on asking God for blessings, or are you truly seeking the understanding to handle what He's already given you?
2. In what areas of your life have you made decisions without first asking God for insight and discernment?
3. Are you willing to pause and pursue understanding, even if it means letting go of what seems urgent or desirable?

Daily Prayer: Dear Lord, give me an understanding heart. Teach me to value insight above riches, honour, or applause. Help me to discern between good and evil, and grant me wisdom to lead, build, and make decisions that please You. In Jesus' name, Amen.

Read the Bible in One Year: 2 Chronicles 17-18; John 13

SEPTEMBER 13

THE HIDDEN COST OF MISUNDERSTANDING

"Man that is in honour, and understandeth not, is like the beasts that perish." Psalm 49:20

The lack of understanding is more expensive than you think. It does not send an invoice upfront, but the charges show up over time: failed relationships, repeated mistakes, wasted years, and missed opportunities.

Our memory verse warns, *"Man that is in honour, and understandeth not, is like the beasts that perish."* You can carry honour and still perish if you lack understanding. That is the danger: it is not always sin that destroys; sometimes it is ignorance. Understanding is not just for big decisions; it is for everyday life. Many people pray, fast, and attend church, yet remain stuck, not because God is silent, but because they lack insight. Without understanding, you misinterpret divine instructions, mishandle relationships, and mismanage seasons. You may be sitting on untapped potential like a man in a car who does not know how the ignition works, pressing buttons but going nowhere. Even Jesus rebuked His disciples, asking, *"Are ye also yet without understanding?"* (Matthew 15:16). These were men walking with Him daily, yet still confused. That is a sobering truth: proximity to power does not equal clarity. Marriages fail, not from lack of love, but lack of understanding. Friendships turn sour because of misread intentions. Spiritual warfare wears you out because you do not understand your authority in Christ. Here is the call: stop pretending to understand what you have not grasped. Ask questions. Pursue wisdom. Seek clarity. Understanding is not automatic; it is a pursuit. You are a king. Do not just wear the crown; learn how to carry it well. Your destiny depends not on how much you know, but how well you understand what you have been given.

Quote of the Day: Your destiny depends not on how much you know, but how well you understand what you have been given.

PERSONAL RESPONSE

1. Have you been mistaking effort for progress in an area of your life where understanding is actually what's missing?
2. What are some recurring frustrations in your life that may be pointing to a lack of clarity or insight?
3. Are you actively seeking to grow in understanding through study, wise counsel, or asking honest questions or have you been pretending to know what you have not yet grasped?

Daily Prayer: Dear Lord, open my eyes to see where I lack understanding. Deliver me from the cycles caused by ignorance. Give me the humility to learn and the hunger to seek wisdom. Let your light flood every area of confusion in my life, and teach me how to walk in the fullness of the honour You have placed on me, in Jesus' name, Amen.

Read the Bible in One Year: 2 Chronicles 19-20

SEPTEMBER 14

THE PATHWAY TO WISDOM Part 1

"The Lord gives wisdom; from his mouth come knowledge and understanding."
Proverbs 2:6

Wisdom is the crown jewel of the kingdom life. But according to Proverbs 4:7, the road to wisdom runs through understanding. You cannot walk in wisdom without it. **Our memory verse** gives the divine flow: *"The Lord gives wisdom; from his mouth come knowledge and understanding."* Think of it like this:

Knowledge + Understanding = Wisdom.

Knowledge tells you *what* something is. Understanding explains the *why* and *how*. Wisdom is the ability to apply both in real life. You may know that fire burns (knowledge), and why it burns (understanding), but wisdom says: *Don't touch it.* This is why many people, though full of scriptures and sermons, still make poor choices. They have knowledge but lack understanding. And without understanding, wisdom remains out of reach.

We live in a generation flooded with information but starving for understanding. Excitement cannot replace it, neither can proximity to truth. Until you sit with what you know and seek clarity, you won't walk in wisdom.

Understanding requires humility, reflection, and pursuit. It reveals the root behind your patterns, why you overspend, why your relationships fail, why your growth stalls. Until you get it, you will keep repeating cycles.

Solomon asked for an understanding heart, and God gave him wisdom. That is the order. So ask yourself, What do I know but not yet understand? What truths have I heard but not applied? Seek understanding. Pray for it. Apply it. That is the pathway to wisdom. That is how kings live.

Quote of the Day: Until you sit with what you know and seek clarity, you won't walk in wisdom.

PERSONAL RESPONSE:

1. What area of your life do you have knowledge in, but lack true understanding; and how has that affected your decisions?
2. Have you been substituting excitement or activity for deep understanding? How can you begin to seek clarity instead?
3. What is one truth God has been showing you repeatedly that you've not yet taken time to fully understand and apply?

Daily Prayer: Dear Lord, give me an understanding heart. Help me not just to know Your Word but to understand it deeply. Let Your Spirit of wisdom and understanding rest on me, guiding my thoughts, decisions, and actions. Teach me how to apply what I learn, so I may walk in true wisdom and reign as You have called me to. In Jesus' name, Amen.

Read the Bible in One Year: 2 Chronicles 21-22; John 14

SEPTEMBER 15

THE PATHWAY TO WISDOM Part 2

"In the first year of his reign I Daniel understood by books the number of the years, whereof the word of the Lord came to Jeremiah the prophet, that he would accomplish seventy years in the desolations of Jerusalem." Daniel 9:2

Yesterday, we explored the equation: Knowledge + Understanding = Wisdom. Today, let us bring that truth to life through the example of Daniel.

Daniel was not an ordinary man. He was wise, favoured, and gifted in interpreting dreams and visions. Yet, despite his prophetic insight and angelic encounters, he remained a student. In Daniel 9:2, he said:

"I, Daniel, understood by books the number of the years…"

He did not rely on supernatural experiences alone. He read. He studied. He came across the writings of Jeremiah and discovered that the seventy-year desolation of Jerusalem was coming to an end. That understanding birthed prophetic intercession. He turned to God in fasting and prayer because he knew what time it was in the spirit.

This was not just curiosity; it was divine alignment. Daniel discerned God's move not by guessing but by searching the Scriptures. Even in Babylon, surrounded by luxury and idolatry, he did not let comfort silence his hunger for God's Word. Daniel models the life of a true king. Kings search for what is written. They do not trade study for spirituality; they embrace both. You can be anointed and still read. You can hear from God and still need understanding. Daniel teaches us that spiritual encounters complement study, not replace it.

God speaks through dreams and visions, but understanding what He has said requires you to seek out what is written. Like Daniel, you must learn to interpret divine timings by diving deep into God's Word.

Understanding is what turns revelation into responsibility. That is how kings rise.

Quote of the Day: Understanding is what turns revelation into responsibility. That is how kings rise.

PERSONAL RESPONSE

1. Are you actively pursuing understanding, or have you been relying only on spiritual experiences without deep study of God's Word?
2. When last did you sit down to search the Scriptures for answers to what you are currently facing?
3. What practical steps can you take this week to grow in understanding?

Daily Prayer: Dear Lord, give me a heart like Daniel's. Help me not to settle for mere knowledge, but to search deeply until I see clearly and walk in wisdom. In Jesus' name, Amen.

Read the Bible in One Year: 2 Chronicles 23-24; John 15

SEPTEMBER 16

THE PATHWAY TO WISDOM Part 3

"And Philip ran thither to him, and heard him read the prophet Esaias, and said, Understandest thou what thou readest?" Acts 8:30

The Ethiopian eunuch offers a powerful picture of how knowledge becomes wisdom only through understanding. A royal treasurer under Queen Candace of Ethiopia, he had access to Scripture. He was reading Isaiah in his chariot, yet something vital was missing.

Philip, led by the Spirit, approached and asked: *"Understandest thou what thou readest?"* (Acts 8:30). This question exposes the heart of the matter. It is not enough to read. The power lies in understanding. The eunuch responded honestly: *"How can I, except some man should guide me?"* (Acts 8:31). He was not ashamed to admit his need. That is the posture of royalty: humility and hunger.

Philip explained the Scriptures, connected them to Christ, and suddenly, the eunuch understood. He immediately asked to be baptized. That moment of understanding unlocked his destiny. He went on his way rejoicing, a changed man. And through him, the gospel entered Africa. Revival began not with knowledge alone, but with knowledge and understanding.

Now compare this to the Daniel example which we looked at yesterday. Daniel too had access to prophetic scrolls. He studied the writings of Jeremiah and "understood by books" what season it was (Daniel 9:2). That understanding birthed intercession and alignment with God's agenda.

Whether it is Daniel searching or the eunuch being taught, the principle is the same: understanding unlocks destiny. Kings do not just skim truth; they seek clarity. They ask questions. They press in. They value understanding.

So ask yourself, Are you willing to be taught like the eunuch? Are you committed to study like Daniel? Wisdom requires understanding, and that is how kings are made.

Quote of the Day: It is not enough to read. The power lies in understanding.

PERSONAL RESPONSE

1. Do you genuinely understand what you read in Scripture, or do you often settle for surface-level familiarity?
2. Are you humble enough to seek guidance when you lack clarity, or do pride and appearances hold you back from deeper understanding?
3. What steps are you taking to turn your knowledge of God's word into practical wisdom for daily living?

Daily Prayer: Heavenly Father, give me a heart that hungers for true understanding. Deliver me from pride, from superficial reading, and from settling for information without revelation. Open my eyes to Your truth, and connect me with the people, teachings, and insights that will unlock my destiny. In Jesus' name, amen.

Read the Bible in One Year: 2 Chronicles 25-27; John 16

SEPTEMBER 17

KINGS SEARCH FOR UNDERSTANDING

"It is the glory of God to conceal a thing: but the honour of kings is to search out a matter." Proverbs 25:2

True kings do not assume; they inquire. Throughout Scripture, we find powerful rulers who, despite their authority, actively searched for understanding. Their examples show us that wisdom is not a luxury for royalty; it is a necessity.

Nebuchadnezzar, king of Babylon, had a troubling dream that none of his magicians could interpret. Rather than ignore it or pretend to understand, he urgently sought answers, even threatening death to those who could not help. Ultimately, he turned to Daniel, a Hebrew exile, who revealed and interpreted the dream through divine insight. Nebuchadnezzar's desperation underscores this truth: kings pursue understanding, no matter the cost. Pharaoh, ruler of Egypt, also had mysterious dreams that baffled his wise men. In a surprising move, he summoned Joseph, a Hebrew prisoner. Pharaoh recognized that Joseph, though lowly in status, had access to divine interpretation. By humbling himself to receive from an unlikely source, Pharaoh saved a nation from famine. Darius, king of Persia, exemplified this pursuit in Ezra 6:1. Faced with a critical decision about the Israelites' temple rebuilding, he ordered a search through the royal archives. That search uncovered King Cyrus's original decree, leading Darius to affirm the Jews' right to build. His diligence brought clarity and alignment with God's purposes. In all three cases, these kings teach us that understanding is an active pursuit. They did not let pride or protocol stop them from seeking truth. Whether through divine messengers, forgotten scrolls, or imprisoned prophets, they searched and found. You, too, are called to be a king. Do not coast on assumptions. Follow the example of kings who searched until they understood. Your destiny depends on what you are willing to seek.

Quote of the Day: Your destiny depends on what you are willing to seek.

PERSONAL RESPONSE:

1. What areas of your life have you left to assumption rather than seeking God for understanding?
2. Are you humble enough to learn from unexpected or unlikely sources, like Pharaoh and Nebuchadnezzar were?
3. How actively are you searching for divine insight before making major decisions

Daily Prayer: Lord, give me the heart of a true king: one that searches for understanding. Deliver me from pride, haste, and assumptions. Teach me to inquire, to listen, and to pursue Your wisdom in every matter of life, no matter how small or great. In Jesus' name, Amen.

Read the Bible in One Year: 2 Chronicles 28-29; John 17

SEPTEMBER 18

UNDERSTANDING AS THE FOUNDATION FOR LIVING ROYALLY

"Why should fools have money in hand to buy wisdom, when they are not able to understand it?" Proverbs 17:16 (NIV)

To live as royalty in Christ is to make understanding foundational. Kingship is not merely a title; it is a responsibility. Without understanding, royalty is reduced to empty position, lacking the wisdom and insight necessary to reign effectively. Understanding is not optional; it is essential. To rule well, a king must be able to interpret times, make wise decisions, and lead with clarity. Likewise, as believers and kings in Christ, we must pursue understanding with intentionality. It affects how we relate to our families, handle finances, build relationships, and steward our faith.

Proverbs 23:23 declares: *"Buy the truth, and sell it not; also wisdom, and instruction, and understanding."* This is a call to treasure truth, to acquire understanding as a possession not to be traded away. It is not for display, but for application. Kings are learners. They do not coast on inherited titles; they equip themselves with knowledge and understanding. As a believer, your car, bedroom, kitchen, and even bathroom can become classrooms. Podcasts, books, Scripture, and sermons must become part of your daily consumption. The more understanding you gain, the more effectively you live as royalty. Our memory verse warns: *"Why should fools have money in hand to buy wisdom, when they are not able to understand it?"* Resources are wasted without understanding. A king with wealth but no wisdom will fail. But a believer with understanding brings order, direction, and divine solutions into every sphere of life. To live royally is to live with clarity. Understanding turns purpose into action and calling into impact. When you make understanding your foundation, you live not just as one who reigns but as one who reigns well.

Quote of the Day: The more understanding you gain, the more effectively you live as royalty.

PERSONAL RESPONSE:

1. In what areas of your life are you currently operating with knowledge but lacking understanding?
1. Are you intentionally creating learning spaces in your daily life to grow in wisdom and insight?
2. How does the way you steward your influence reflect your commitment to understanding?
3. What changes can you make today to prioritize the pursuit of truth, wisdom, and understanding in your walk with God?

Daily Prayer: Dear Lord, give me a deep hunger for understanding. Teach me to value truth above convenience, and to pursue wisdom in every area of life. Let my kingship in Christ be marked by clarity, discernment, and purpose. Open my eyes to see, my heart to perceive, and my mind to retain what truly matters. May I reign with insight and lead with understanding, bringing glory to Your name. Amen.

Read the Bible in One Year: 2 Chronicles 30-31; John 18

LEARNING AS A LIFELONG REQUIREMENT FOR KINGS

"If thou seekest her as silver, and searchest for her as for hid treasures; Then shalt thou understand the fear of the Lord, and find the knowledge of God." Proverbs 2:4-5

Royals require a training that fits their calling. Queen Elizabeth II, for example, was groomed with specialized lessons to prepare her for rulership. In the same way, as a royal in Christ, your learning must be intentional and ongoing.

Learning is not a one-time achievement; it is a lifestyle. Kings never stop growing. They seek wisdom beyond the classroom, knowing that the demands of their destiny evolve with time. Your purpose requires continuous development; spiritually, mentally, and emotionally. Scripture affirms this: *"You will seek Me and find Me when you seek Me with all your heart."* (Jeremiah 29:13). *"Ask…seek…knock…"* (Matthew 7:7). Wisdom is reserved for the diligent, not the passive. Proverbs 2:1–6 urges us to pursue wisdom like hidden treasure. This is the royal posture. Biblical kings modelled this. Saul was mentored by Samuel. David was guided by prophets. Elisha advised kings. Mentorship and prophetic instruction were essential to their reign. The same must be true for you. Learn from others. Seek counsel. Embrace correction. Ask yourself: When last did I intentionally invest in my growth? Reading sharpens your mind like exercise strengthens the body. When you stop learning, you start declining. The world keeps evolving, and so must you.

As a royal in Christ, cultivate a lifestyle of learning. Read books. Attend trainings. Engage mentors. Listen to truth. Stretch your understanding. Kings are not made by titles; they are made by training. And that training never ends. To live royally is to learn continually.

Quote of the Day: Kings are not made by titles; they are made by training. And that training never ends.

PERSONAL RESPONSE

1. What specific areas of your life currently demand a fresh investment in learning or growth?
2. When was the last time you submitted to mentorship or deliberately sought instruction? What was the result?
3. Are you actively building a lifestyle of learning, or are you coasting on past knowledge?

Daily Prayer: Dear Lord, give me the hunger and humility to learn continually. Help me never outgrow my need for wisdom, instruction, and understanding. Make me teachable and diligent, and connect me to the voices You have assigned to train me for my royal assignment. In Jesus' name. Amen.

Read the Bible in One Year: 2 Chronicles 32-33

SEPTEMBER 20

THE HUNGER THAT UNLOCKS MYSTERIES

"And the disciples came, and said unto him, Why speakest thou unto them in parables?" Matthew 13:10

In the passage quoted above, the disciples asked Jesus, *"Why do you speak to the people in parables?"* Their question revealed two royal traits: hunger and humility. True kings ask questions. They acknowledge that they do not know everything and actively pursue understanding. This hunger to understand is what unlocks mysteries. It is not enough to know facts; kings seek meaning. Wisdom is your royal inheritance in Christ, but to access it, you must desire it. Hunger is the key. When you are truly hungry, you will go the extra mile to learn, grow, and discover truth. Learning begins with humility. A king who cannot admit ignorance cannot gain wisdom. True royalty is teachable, constantly asking, seeking, and growing. Kings are solution providers, and that requires curiosity and a learning mindset. Jesus said, *"Ask, and it shall be given you; seek, and ye shall find… "* (Matthew 7:7). If you are willing to learn, there is no limit to how far you can grow. Life's mysteries are not beyond your reach when you are hungry to understand. But this requires intentional learning. "Heavy consumption" is not about mindless content but meaningful growth. Choose books, teachings, and resources that stretch you and align with your divine assignment. If you feed only on entertainment, do not expect royal results. Entertainment may refresh, but it does not equip. The principle is simple: You grow by what you consume. If you want to live royally, consume wisely. Be discerning. Be intentional. Your royal destiny depends on it. As your hunger grows, understanding will increase. Mysteries will unfold. Your life will be shaped by revelation, and that is how kings are made.

Quote of the Day: You grow by what you consume. If you want to live royally, consume wisely. Be discerning. Be intentional. Your royal destiny depends on it.

PERSONAL RESPONSE:

1. Are you truly hungry for understanding, or have you settled for surface-level knowledge?
2. When was the last time you asked a question or sought clarity about something you didn't understand?
3. Are you intentional about the content you consume, or are you feeding your mind with things that do not align with your calling?

Daily Prayer: Dear Lord, stir up a deep hunger for understanding in me. Help me to be teachable, discerning, and intentional with what I consume. Let my pursuit of wisdom unlock the mysteries I need to fulfil my purpose. In Jesus' name, I pray. Amen.

Read the Bible in One Year: 2 Chronicles 34-36; John 19

THE VALUE OF DOCUMENTING REVELATION

"And the Lord answered me, and said, Write the vision, and make it plain upon tables, that he may run that readeth it." Habakkuk 2:2

Great men and women do not just receive insight; they also write it down. From ancient kings to modern thinkers, documentation has marked those who walk in wisdom. Why? Because what you do not write, you forget. And what you forget, you cannot apply. Writing is not just recording; it is honouring revelation. It shows God that you value what He says.

If you do not write things down, it simply means you do not value them. Nations keep constitutions. God told Moses to write. The very existence of the Bible is proof of the power of documentation. Jesus told John, "Write the things which thou hast seen." When you document revelation, you preserve it. And when you honour it, God entrusts you with more.

The church is not a social hall but a spiritual university. Every sermon, every whisper in prayer, every insight in devotion is a potential key. But keys not kept are easily lost. How many life-changing messages have you forgotten because you failed to write them down? Jesus said in Matthew 13:11: *"It is given unto you to know the mysteries of the kingdom of heaven."* But mysteries are revealed to those who seek, and seekers write.

Think of your journal as a vault. If God speaks today and you do not capture it, what assurance do you have He will speak more tomorrow? But when you write, you create a spiritual archive, a personal library of divine instruction.

So, keep a journal. Take sermon notes. Revisit them. Do not treat revelation lightly. Write it down, and watch God trust you with more.

Quote of the Day: When you document revelation, you preserve it. And when you honour it, God entrusts you with more.

PERSONAL RESPONSE

1. Do you consistently write down the insights and instructions God gives you, or have you allowed powerful revelations to slip away through neglect?
2. What steps can you take this week to begin cultivating a habit of documenting what God is teaching you?
3. Have you treated your notes from sermons, devotionals, or personal study as treasures worth revisiting, or have they simply gathered dust?

Daily Prayer: Dear Lord, give me a disciplined heart that values every word You speak to me. Help me to treasure, document, and revisit Your revelations so that I may grow in wisdom and live faithfully according to Your will. In Jesus' name, Amen.

Read the Bible in One Year: Ezra 1-2

PURSUING UNDERSTANDING IN THE PRACTICAL MATTERS OF LIFE

"My people are destroyed for lack of knowledge: because thou hast rejected knowledge, I will also reject thee, that thou shalt be no priest to me: seeing thou hast forgotten the law of thy God, I will also forget thy children." Hosea 4:6

One of the most vital places to apply your kingly pursuit of understanding is in the practical matters of life such as marriage, money, parenting, healing, etc. These areas shape your daily experience and long-term impact. Yet many believers treat them lightly, relying on love to sustain a marriage or hard work to build wealth. But kings do not operate by assumption; they seek insight in every area that affects their dominion. Take marriage, for instance. How long do you want it to last? What quality are you aiming for? Have you studied communication, conflict resolution, or companionship? Many homes fail not for lack of love, but lack of understanding. Intentions are not enough; wisdom is essential. The same applies to parenting. Each child is unique. Parenting cannot be outsourced. As a king, you are shaping destinies. That demands learning. If you have not studied how to raise godly, emotionally healthy children, you are gambling with the future you have been called to secure. What about finances? Schools teach math but rarely teach how to manage money. Yet you are called to multiply and steward resources. Without understanding, money slips through your hands. Our text says, *"My people are destroyed for lack of knowledge."* Not because of the devil but ignorance. Even healing requires understanding. God is our Healer, but how well do you understand divine health? Have you studied rest, diet, and stress management? Without understanding, we suffer needlessly. Proverbs 25:2 says, *"It is the glory of God to conceal a matter; to search out a matter is the glory of kings."* Seekers dig for wisdom; spectators wait for it to fall. As a king, you do not wait. You read, ask, and learn. Because anywhere you lack understanding, you will be limited.

Quote of the Day: Seekers dig for wisdom; spectators wait for it to fall. As a king, you do not wait. You read, ask, and learn. Because anywhere you lack understanding, you will be limited.

PERSONAL RESPONSE:

1. In which practical area of your life do you most need to grow in understanding right now?
2. Have you been assuming that good intentions alone are enough, or have you been intentional about learning and seeking wisdom in that area?
3. What step will you take this week to pursue understanding?

Daily Prayer: Dear Lord, give me a hunger for understanding in every area of my life. Help me not to walk in ignorance or assumption, but to actively seek wisdom so I can fulfil my royal assignment with excellence and impact. In Jesus' name, I pray. Amen.

Read the Bible in One Year: Ezra 3-5; John 20

SEPTEMBER 23

KINGS SEEK SUBSTANCE, NOT JUST RESULTS

"Give therefore thy servant an understanding heart to judge thy people, that I may discern between good and bad: for who is able to judge this thy so great a people?" 1 Kings 3:9

When Solomon made his request to God, he could have asked for riches or long life. Instead, he asked for wisdom, the capacity to lead and judge rightly. He understood that true success flows from substance. If he had wisdom, the rest would follow. That mindset is what made Solomon a reference point for wisdom through the ages.

Kings are not driven by surface-level cravings. They look beneath the results and pursue the ingredients that produce lasting impact. Solomon's choice was not glamorous, but it revealed what mattered to him: being a better ruler, not just appearing prosperous. That is the difference between kings and common men. True kings understand that the right substance produces the right results. Wisdom, understanding, and insight are the raw materials that establish dominion. Kings do not chase applause; they chase answers. Their strength lies not in possessions, but in perception. Imagine a wealthy man giving you money versus teaching you to create wealth. One is temporary relief; the other, lasting empowerment. One is a gift; the other, a legacy. Kings always go for the latter. This is why Solomon stands out. He did not ask for what would make him look powerful; he asked for what would make him be powerful. His greatness was not in wealth alone, but in the wisdom, governance, and peace he brought to Israel.

Kings think generationally. They invest in what outlives them. Their focus is deeper than results; it is about the roots. Solomon's prayer teaches us a vital lesson: Do not just chase outcomes. Pursue the substance that creates them.

Quote of the Day: Do not just chase outcomes. Pursue the substance that creates them.

PERSONAL RESPONSE:

1. What do you find yourself pursuing more often?
2. Have you prioritized short-term gains over building the lasting substance God wants to develop in you?
3. What specific areas of your life require a shift from chasing appearances to cultivating depth and substance?

Daily Prayer: Dear Lord, teach me to value substance over results. Help me not to crave the applause of men but to seek the wisdom, insight, and understanding that will equip me for lasting impact. Make me a king who carries what truly matters. In Jesus' name, I pray. Amen.

Read the Bible in One Year: Ezra 6-8; John 21

SEPTEMBER 24

THE ROYAL CURRENCY

"Counsel is mine, and sound wisdom: I am understanding; I have strength. By me kings reign, and princes decree justice." Proverbs 8:14–15

In our memory verse above, wisdom speaks with divine authority: "By me kings reign." Not by wealth, title, or might, but by wisdom. It is the true currency of kingship. It empowers rulers to lead with clarity, govern with justice, and make decisions that shape destinies. Without wisdom, crowns mean little. Leadership becomes fragile and hollow.

Solomon understood this. That was why, when given the chance to ask for anything, he asked for wisdom. Not riches. Not revenge. Not power. He knew that without understanding, his reign would collapse. That prayer unlocked a legacy, making him the wisest king in history. He did not just write about wisdom; he wore it like a robe. As believers, Revelation 5:10 says God has made us kings and priests. But functioning as royalty requires more than identity; it requires wisdom. Many are royal by calling but ineffective in expression because they lack understanding. Wisdom turns position into power. That is why Proverbs 8:17 urges: *"I love them that love me; and those that seek me early shall find me."*

Timing matters. Seek wisdom early before battles arise, before crises explode, before doors close. Delayed pursuit often leads to missed opportunities and preventable pain. Kings do not wait for trouble before seeking counsel. They study, prepare, and lean into understanding before urgency demands it. Wisdom pays for influence, stability, and legacy. It brings clarity in confusion and solutions where others see problems. If you want to reign with honour, treasure wisdom. Let it be your most prized possession because while your crown may be spiritual, your reign will be sustained by insight.

Quote of the Day: If you want to reign with honour, treasure wisdom. Let it be your most prized possession because while your crown may be spiritual, your reign will be sustained by insight.

PERSONAL RESPONSE:

1. Do you truly value wisdom as the foundation for reigning in life, or have you been relying more on talent, position, or charisma?
2. In what specific areas of your life are you currently operating without the depth of understanding that wisdom provides?
3. What intentional steps will you take this week to seek wisdom early, before challenges arise?

Daily Prayer: Dear Lord, give me a heart that treasures wisdom above all else. Help me to seek You early, to value Your counsel, and to walk in understanding that I may reign with honour and fulfil my calling. Let me never chase results without first possessing the substance that produces them. In Jesus' name, I pray. Amen.

Read the Bible in One Year: Ezra 9-10; Acts 1

SEPTEMBER 25

THE TREASURES WISDOM DELIVERS

"Riches and honour are with me; yea, durable riches and righteousness... that I may cause those that love me to inherit substance; and I will fill their treasures." Proverbs 8:18–21

These are not promises from a motivational speaker; they are the voice of wisdom itself. Wisdom offers what many people spend their entire lives chasing: riches, honour, righteousness, and substance. That is why, while the world runs after results, real kings pursue wisdom. And in doing so, they receive everything wisdom carries.

Many chase business ideas, titles, and relationships hoping for breakthrough. But kings do not chase shadows; they seek substance. Wisdom is the womb from which lasting success is born. It brings riches that last, honour that is not dependent on applause, and righteousness that anchors your prosperity in integrity. It fills your life with treasure that does not vanish in crisis.

But here is the key: the wise do not pursue wisdom merely for what it can give. They value wisdom for who she is. Kings rejoice in her presence even before the fruit appears. This posture is what marks royalty.

Proverbs 24:3–4 reveals wisdom's architecture: *"Through wisdom is an house builded; and by understanding it is established: and by knowledge shall the chambers be filled..."* Wisdom builds, understanding establishes, and knowledge fills.

In a world of instability, Isaiah 33:6 declares: *"Wisdom and knowledge shall be the stability of thy times."* Trends and talents shift, but wisdom anchors.

Let others chase rewards. Kings chase wisdom. And by doing so, they receive both the treasure and the capacity to steward it well.

Quote of the Day: Wisdom is the womb from which lasting success is born.

PERSONAL RESPONSE:

1. Are you currently pursuing wisdom for who she is, or only for what she can give you?
2. In which area of your life have you been chasing results instead of seeking the wisdom that produces them?
3. What steps can you take this week to value wisdom more intentionally, through reading, mentorship, or prayerful study?

Daily Prayer: Dear Lord, give me a heart that treasures wisdom above results. Help me to pursue understanding, not just for gain, but because I value Your ways. Fill me with the kind of wisdom that builds, establishes, and sustains every part of my life. In Jesus' name, I pray. Amen.

Read the Bible in One Year: Nehemiah 1-3

THE NATURE OF KINGS 1: COUNSEL

"Where no counsel is, the people fall: but in the multitude of counsellors there is safety." Proverbs 11:14

A consistent pattern runs through the Scriptures we have explored in the last few days (Proverbs 8, Proverbs 24, Isaiah 33, 1 Kings 3 and 4). Six spiritual traits define those who function as kings: **wisdom, knowledge, understanding, counsel, largeness of heart, and discernment.** These are not optional; they are the fabric of true rulership.

We have already examined wisdom, knowledge, and understanding. Now we turn to the remaining three, beginning with **counsel.** In Scripture, the Hebrew word for counsel, *etsah,* speaks of purposeful guidance and well-formed plans. Kings are not omniscient; they rise or fall by the voices they choose to heed. King Rehoboam, Solomon's son, offers a compelling example (1 Kings 12). When the people asked for relief from his father's heavy burdens, Rehoboam first consulted the elders who had advised Solomon. They recommended kindness and understanding. But Rehoboam also sought counsel from his peers, who urged him to rule harshly. He rejected the elders' wisdom and followed his peers' prideful advice. The result? The kingdom split, and he lost ten tribes in a single moment of misjudgment. This reveals a sobering truth: **counsel can be the hinge of a king's destiny.** The difference between stability and collapse often lies in the advice one chooses to follow. Psalm 33:11 says, *"The counsel of the Lord stands forever…"* If even God works through counsel, how much more should kings? Seeking wise counsel is not weakness; it is humility in strength.

Sadly, many today resist advice. Yet Proverbs 11:14 reminds us, *"In the multitude of counsellors, there is safety."* Kings do not rule alone; they surround themselves with wisdom.

Quote of the Day: The difference between stability and collapse often lies in the advice one chooses to follow.

PERSONAL RESPONSE

1. Whose counsel are you currently listening to in key areas of your life? Are they wise, godly voices or just familiar ones?
2. Have you cultivated the humility to seek advice, or do you tend to rely only on your instincts and past experiences?
3. What steps will you take this week to surround yourself with counsellors who fear God and speak truth, even when it is uncomfortable?

Daily Prayer: Lord, give me the humility to seek wise counsel and the discernment to recognise Your voice in the midst of many opinions. Help me to walk in the safety that comes from godly advice and not in the pride of self-reliance. In Jesus' name, Amen.

Read the Bible in One Year: Nehemiah 4-6; Acts 2

SEPTEMBER 27

THE NATURE OF KINGS 2: LARGENESS OF HEART

"And God gave Solomon wisdom and understanding exceeding much, and largeness of heart, even as the sand that is on the seashore." 1 Kings 4:29

When God equips a man to reign, He gives more than wisdom. He also gives *largeness of heart.* This was true of Solomon, as seen in our text above.

Largeness of heart is no ordinary gift. It is divine enablement that allows a man to carry more, think bigger, and act beyond the limits of fear, selfishness, or small vision. When Solomon prayed for wisdom, God gave him capacity to match. Wisdom without space to contain it leads to waste. But largeness of heart gives wisdom room to work. Kings need this. They must think in terms of generations, not just days; nations, not just neighbourhoods. Petty spirits cannot reign well. Kings must carry burdens, embrace people, and steward weighty matters with grace. To be enlarged is to be stretched for purpose. It means being made big enough to handle what God wants to entrust. Without it, blessing can become a burden. Jabez understood this when he prayed: *"Oh that thou wouldest bless me indeed, and enlarge my coast…" 1 Chronicles 4:10*

He was not just asking for more land, but for internal capacity. And God granted his request.

Largeness of heart is not automatic. You must desire it. And when God sees your readiness, He stretches you. He enlarges your inner room so He can increase your outer influence.

This is the nature of kings. They do not lead with small hearts or tight spirits. They are open to God, open to growth, and open to people. And as their hearts grow, so does their impact.

Quote of the Day: When God equips a man to reign, He gives more than wisdom. He also gives *largeness of heart.*

PERSONAL RESPONSE:

1. Are you willing to let God stretch your heart so you can carry more than just your own needs and concerns?
2. In what areas of your life have you sensed a need for greater capacity emotionally, spiritually, or in leadership?
3. Do you sometimes resist growth because of the discomfort it brings, or are you ready to embrace the stretching that leads to enlargement?

Daily Prayer: Dear Lord, enlarge my heart and stretch my capacity. Help me not to shrink from growth or resist the weight of responsibility You want to entrust to me. Make me big enough within to carry the fullness of Your calling on my life. In Jesus' name, I pray. Amen.

Read the Bible in One Year: Nehemiah 7-9; Acts 3

SEPTEMBER 28

THE NATURE OF KINGS 3: DISCERNMENT

"Give therefore thy servant an understanding heart to judge thy people, that I may discern between good and bad: for who is able to judge this thy so great a people?" 1 Kings 3:9

Discernment is a royal necessity. A king without it is like a warrior without eyes. He is vulnerable, easily deceived, and prone to costly mistakes. Discernment is what enables kings to judge righteously, navigate wisely, and lead effectively in a world full of noise and deception. Rehoboam, son of Solomon, had the throne but lacked discernment. He ignored wise counsel and followed reckless advice from his peers. That singular failure split the kingdom and marked the beginning of national decline. He was a king, but he did not discern like one. Discernment empowers kings in four critical areas:

1. To Judge People Rightly: Samuel almost anointed Eliab king based on appearance, but God corrected him: *"Man looketh on the outward appearance, but the Lord looketh on the heart"* (1 Samuel 16:7). Kings must see beyond appearances.

2. To Separate Sin from Duty: Some things seem right but are subtle distractions. Discernment helps kings avoid moral compromises that are culturally acceptable but spiritually wrong.

3. To Detect Deception: Not all spiritual-sounding messages are true. Discernment allows a king to sense error even when it is beautifully packaged, testing all things against God's Word.

4. To Choose What Is Truly Good: Discernment enables kings to reject glittering but deadly options, anchoring their decisions in divine standards rather than shifting feelings.

Discernment is not automatic; it must be pursued. Like Solomon, you must ask for it. Like David, you must cultivate it in God's presence. Kings lead by light, not guesswork.

Quote of the Day: Kings lead by light, not guesswork.

PERSONAL RESPONSE:

1. Are you more inclined to judge situations and people by outward appearances, or do you pause to seek discernment from the Lord?
2. In what specific area of your life do you currently need discernment to avoid error and make wise decisions?
3. Have you been actively cultivating discernment through prayer, Scripture, and intimacy with God, or have you been relying mostly on instinct and emotion?

Daily Prayer: Dear Lord, sharpen my discernment. Teach me to see what You see, hear what You are saying, and choose what truly pleases You. Deliver me from deception and help me to walk in light, in wisdom, and in truth. In Jesus' name, I pray. Amen.

Read the Bible in One Year: Nehemiah 10-11; Acts 4

SEPTEMBER 29

THE RENEWED MIND AS THE KEY TO ROYAL LIVING

"And be not conformed to this world: but be ye transformed by the renewing of your mind, that ye may prove what is that good, and acceptable, and perfect, will of God." Romans 12:2

The true battle for kingship is fought in the mind. You cannot walk in royalty while thinking in shame, fear, or unworthiness. That is why God begins your transformation by renewing your mind, not by changing your clothes or titles. Our text says, *"Be ye transformed by the renewing of your mind..."* Transformation does not come by a change in environment or external activities, but by the daily renovation of thought. You cannot reign in life if your mind remains bound. Many believers are spiritually active but mentally stuck. They pray, serve, and quote Scripture, yet their thinking is ruled by insecurity and self-doubt. A king without a renewed mind is like a warrior without strength. Royalty begins when your thoughts align with your identity in Christ. To think royally is to show up with confidence, knowing you were sent by God. It is not arrogance; it is divine assurance. You stop shrinking back and start saying, *"If God sent me, nothing is impossible."* This requires discipline. Just as physical fitness needs repetition, mental transformation demands continual truth. You must reject fear, confront lies, and train your mind to believe what God says about you. A renewed mind produces boldness, clarity, and spiritual authority. Soon, your prayers shift from begging to declaring. You stop asking for permission to exist. You begin walking through doors with confidence, knowing that heaven backs you. You are not an impostor. You are an heir. God is not asking you to pretend; He is asking you to believe. Until your mind is renewed, royalty will feel distant. But once your thoughts change, everything changes. **Let Him renew your mind. That is where royalty begins.**

Quote of the Day: A king without a renewed mind is like a warrior without strength. Royalty begins when your thoughts align with your identity in Christ.

PERSONAL RESPONSE QUESTIONS

1. What lies about your identity have you unknowingly accepted, and how have they affected the way you show up in life?
2. In what areas of your life do you still think like a slave or orphan, rather than as a king and heir in Christ?
3. What practical steps can you take each day to renew your mind with God's truth and strengthen your royal mindset?

Daily Prayer: Dear Lord, renew my mind by Your truth. Uproot every lie I have believed about myself, and establish me in the identity You gave me in Christ. Train my thoughts to align with Your Word, and help me live daily with the confidence, clarity, and courage of a true heir of the Kingdom. In Jesus' name, I pray. Amen.

Read the Bible in One Year: Nehemiah 12-13

SEPTEMBER 30

THE MARK OF KINGSHIP IN THE KINGDOM OF GOD

"And whosoever of you will be the chiefest, shall be servant of all." Mark 10:44

In God's Kingdom, kingship is not about how many serve you; it is about how many you serve. This confronts the world's definition of greatness. While earthly rulers chase position, applause, and power, Jesus flipped the script: true royalty is found in being poured out. This is not a suggestion; it is Kingdom protocol. You are called to reign, but your reign must uplift others. In Christ, kings do not climb over people to ascend; they lift others as they rise.

Jesus, the greatest King, washed feet, fed the hungry, healed the sick, and gave His life for the undeserving. *Philippians 2:5–11* reveals this servant mindset:

"Let this mind be in you, which was also in Christ Jesus..."

Jesus emptied Himself, took the form of a servant, and humbled Himself to death. That is why God exalted Him.

The crown and the towel are not enemies; they are companions. Kingdom kings must think and serve like Christ. *1 Corinthians 2:16* says you have His mind. That means you carry the capacity to serve with power, not pride.

If your leadership does not lift others, it is not kingly. If your influence does not serve others, it is not divine. You were not crowned to sit; you were crowned to serve. That is the mark of true royalty.

Quote of the Day: The crown and the towel are not enemies; they are companions. Kingdom kings must think and serve like Christ.

PERSONAL RESPONSE:

1. In what areas of your life have you viewed leadership or influence as a right to be served rather than a call to serve?
2. Whose feet is God calling you to wash right now?
3. How are you using your current position, gifts, or resources to lift others?

Daily Prayer: Dear Lord, give me a heart that does not seek to be served, but to serve. Help me to follow Christ's example of humility, selflessness, and sacrificial love. May I never wear the crown without the towel. Teach me to reign by lifting others. In Jesus' name, amen.

Read the Bible in One Year: Esther 3-5

OCTOBER

WELCOME TO THE MONTH OF SPIRITUAL GROWTH

PROPHETIC DECREE

I decree that this is your month of remarkable spiritual growth, you will not settle for surface Christianity but be drawn into deep intimacy with God. Each day, the Holy Spirit will transform you from within, igniting an unquenchable hunger for His presence. Your life will bear fruit that remains, faithfulness, true obedience, and love beyond words. As shallow roots give way to depth and every fruitless branch is pruned for abundance. You will not be swayed by appearances or measured by the world's standards, for the Lord Himself is your mirror, guide, and source. Your surrender will deepen, your hunger will intensify, and Christ will be fully formed in you. You will live as a testimony to the unstoppable power of true spiritual growth.

SPIRITUAL GROWTH

Welcome to our month of spiritual growth.

Spiritual growth is not a destination; it is a daily invitation to become more like Christ. It is not about becoming busier with religious activities or gathering impressive spiritual experiences. It is about going deeper in intimacy with God, deeper in obedience, deeper in love. This devotional is for anyone who is hungry, not just for more knowledge about God, but for more of God Himself.

Too often, we measure spiritual maturity by outward signs like gifts, achievements, popularity, or productivity. But the Bible is clear: the true sign that you are growing spiritually is that you are bearing fruit. And fruit is not flashy. It is quiet. It grows slowly, steadily, and often in secret. That is why this devotional will not flatter you; it will challenge you. It will call you away from surface Christianity and draw you into the deep waters where real transformation happens. Over the next 31 days, you will be reminded that you cannot grow by self-effort. True growth is the work of the Holy Spirit in a yielded life. We will explore themes like faithfulness, intimacy, and eternity-minded living. Each entry is designed to realign your heart with what matters most. Take your time each day. Read slowly. Reflect deeply. Allow the questions in the personal response section to search your heart, and let the daily prayer anchor your soul. Do not rush through it. Let it read you. Because this is not just a devotional. It is a mirror, a pruning knife, and an invitation to grow.

May these pages awaken hunger, deepen surrender, and stir you to press on until Christ is fully formed in you.

TABLE OF CONTENTS

OCTOBER 01

THE MYSTERY OF RESURRECTION LIFE

"Therefore we are buried with him by baptism into death: that like as Christ was raised up from the dead by the glory of the Father, even so we also should walk in newness of life. For if we have been planted together in the likeness of his death, we shall be also in the likeness of his resurrection." Romans 6:4–5

The passage above declares that just as Christ was raised from the dead, we too should walk in *newness of life.* This is not poetic imagery; it is spiritual truth. When Jesus died, you died. When He rose, you rose. Not in body, but in spirit.

If you read the whole of Romans 6, you would find that it uses both legal and agricultural language: *planted, buried, raised.* Like a seed, your old spirit died. What emerged was not a better version of you, but a completely new creation. *"If any man be in Christ, he is a new creature..."* (2 Corinthians 5:17).

This resurrection is not symbolic; it is real, and it happens in the spirit. Colossians 2:12 affirms that you are risen with Him through faith. The same power that raised Christ also called your spirit to life. That is why Ephesians 2:6 says you've been *raised and seated* with Christ. It is past tense, meaning it is already accomplished. So what is this *newness of life?* It is not self-improvement or routine change. It is the Spirit-energized life of a re-created inner man. But though your spirit is transformed, your body and mind must still be renewed (Romans 12:2). Do not expect instant perfection. Your spirit is saved, but your flesh is not. Feelings may mislead you, but your true identity is secure in Christ. Holiness does not begin with trying harder; it begins with revelation. You grow not by striving but by living from who you now are.

You were crucified with Christ. You are now risen with Him. This is the mystery of resurrection life, and it changes everything.

Quote of the Day: Holiness does not begin with trying harder; it begins with revelation. You grow not by striving but by living from who you now are.

PERSONAL RESPONSE:

1. In what specific ways are you still living as though your old self is alive, instead of walking in the new life you have in Christ?
2. Do you measure your spiritual growth by how you feel, or by what God's Word says about who you are in Christ?
3. What areas of your life still need to come under the leadership of your resurrected spirit?

Daily Prayer: Dear Lord, open my eyes to the reality of my resurrection with Christ. Help me to live from my new identity, not my old habits, and teach me to walk daily in the power of Your Spirit. In Jesus' name, I pray. Amen.

Read the Bible in One Year: Esther 6-8; Acts 6

THE CHRISTIAN LIFE: A SPIRITUAL WALK

"This I say then, Walk in the Spirit, and ye shall not fulfil the lust of the flesh." Galatians 5:16

If your spirit has been raised with Christ as you learnt yesterday, then your Christian life must flow from that spiritual reality. Christianity is not a behavioural religion; it is a spiritual walk. Your growth, battles, and maturity are all rooted in your spirit.

Many believers try to live from the outside in, focusing on church attendance, rules, and appearance. But Christianity is not about polishing the flesh. It is about nurturing the spirit. Our text says, *"Walk in the Spirit, and ye shall not fulfil the lust of the flesh."* The victory begins in the spirit.

Your spirit is the control centre of your Christian life. That is where the Holy Spirit dwells. That is where grace operates. Romans 8:14 says, *"For as many as are led by the Spirit of God, they are the sons of God."* Being led by the Spirit means living from the part of you that is alive to God.

Just as we feed the body and train the mind, we must build the spirit. Jude 20 says, *"Building up yourselves on your most holy faith, praying in the Holy Ghost."* Prayer, study, worship, and obedience are not rituals; they are spiritual exercises. Ephesians 3:16 prays that you be *"strengthened with might by his Spirit in the inner man."* A strong spirit can carry a weary soul. And as your spirit grows, your appetite changes.

The Christian life is not self-improvement. It is living from your new identity in the spirit. Jesus said, *"Out of his belly shall flow rivers of living water"* (John 7:38). That flow comes from your spirit man. And that is the only way to truly walk with God.

Quote of the Day: The Christian life is not self-improvement. It is living from your new identity in the spirit.

PERSONAL RESPONSE:

1. Are you living your Christian life from the outside in, or from the inside out?
2. What habits or distractions are keeping you from feeding and strengthening your spirit man?
3. In what specific areas do you need to shift your focus from self-effort to spiritual alignment?

Daily Prayer: Dear Lord, help me to walk in the Spirit and not rely on my flesh. Teach me to build up my inner man through prayer, your Word, and daily surrender. May my life flow from the strength of your presence within me. In Jesus' name, I pray. Amen.

Read the Bible in One Year: Esther 9-10; Acts 7

UNDERSTANDING YOUR SPIRITUAL ADDRESS

"And hath raised us up together, and made us sit together in heavenly places in Christ Jesus." Ephesians 2:6

Where is your spirit seated right now? Physically, you may be in your house, car, or office, but spiritually, you are seated in heavenly places in Christ Jesus. This is not a metaphor. It is your spiritual reality.

When you believed in Christ, your old self died, and your spirit was raised and seated with Him. Christianity is not about climbing up to God. It is about living from where He has already placed you, beside Christ at the right hand of the Father (see Ephesians 1:20–21). That seat is a place of authority, not struggle. You are not praying from earth hoping to be heard in heaven. You are praying from heaven into the earth. You are not wrestling for victory; you are enforcing it. You are not beneath; you are above. Earth is your assignment, but heaven is your origin, your resource base, and your home. Think of it like having a spiritual bank account. Everything Christ paid for is already credited to you, but to access it, you must know where your account is located.

Colossians 3:1–2 says, *"Seek those things which are above… Set your affection on things above."* Your mind must match your spirit's position. The enemy wants you focused on your earthly condition. But when you remember where you are seated, everything changes. Your seat is secure. Your identity is settled. You are not trying to reach God; you are already in Him. So when fear, doubt, or lies whisper otherwise, ask yourself: **Where am I seated right now?**

Your answer? **In heavenly places, in Christ Jesus.** That is your spiritual address. Never forget it.

Quote of the Day: Christianity is not about climbing up to God. It is about living from where He has already placed you, beside Christ at the right hand of the Father.

PERSONAL RESPONSE

1. How often does your daily mindset reflect your true spiritual position in Christ?
2. In what ways are you still living and praying as though you are beneath, rather than seated above?
3. What practical steps can you take to align your thoughts and actions with your heavenly position?

Daily Prayer: Dear Lord, thank You for raising me up and seating me with Christ in heavenly places. Help me to live each day from that place of victory, authority, and peace. Teach me to see myself as You see me and to walk in the confidence of my true spiritual identity. In Jesus' name, I pray. Amen.

Read the Bible in One Year: Job 1-2

ACCESSING YOUR SPIRITUAL BLESSINGS

"Blessed be the God and Father of our Lord Jesus Christ, who hath blessed us with all spiritual blessings in heavenly places in Christ." Ephesians 1:3

Notice that our text speaks of all spiritual blessings, not a few. And where are they? In heavenly places, in Christ. They are already yours, stored in your spiritual account.

Many believers confuse the biblical concept of blessings with material things like health, wealth, success. In the Old Testament, blessings were often physical. But in Christ, we have received far greater blessings: spiritual ones. These may not always be visible, but they are eternal and far more powerful.

Imagine a beggar girl marrying a prince. She instantly gains access to all he owns, not by working for it, but by union. That is your story. When you were born again, you were joined to Christ. His riches became your inheritance.

So why don't many believers see these blessings? Because access is based on knowledge and faith. Like having money in the bank without knowing your PIN, you cannot enjoy what you do not understand. Faith unlocks your inheritance. You do not earn these blessings through rituals or good behaviour. You receive them by grace, through faith in what Christ has already done.

The more you believe who you are in Christ, the more these blessings shape your reality. Peace replaces anxiety. Joy replaces despair. Power replaces weakness. Stop praying like a beggar. You are not trying to get blessed. You are already blessed. Ask God to open your eyes and teach you to walk in what is yours. This is not striving. This is grace. You have been blessed with all spiritual blessings in Christ. Believe it. Receive it. Walk in it. That is your inheritance. That is your birthright.

Quote of the Day: You are not trying to get blessed. You are already blessed. Ask God to open your eyes and teach you to walk in what is yours.

PERSONAL RESPONSE:

1. Does your daily attitude reflect someone who knows they are already blessed in Christ?
2. What spiritual blessings do you need to stop striving for and start receiving by faith?
3. In what practical ways can you begin to walk in the reality of your inheritance in Christ?

Daily Prayer: Dear Lord, thank You for blessing me with every spiritual blessing in Christ. Help me to stop striving and start receiving. Open my eyes to see what already belongs to me, and teach me to walk in the fullness of Your grace. In Jesus' name, I pray. Amen.

Read the Bible in One Year: Job 3-4

HOW NOT TO JUDGE YOUR SPIRITUAL GROWTH

"O foolish Galatians, who hath bewitched you, that ye should not obey the truth, before whose eyes Jesus Christ hath been evidently set forth, crucified among you? Are ye so foolish? having begun in the Spirit, are ye now made perfect by the flesh?" Galatians 3:1, 3

Many believers wrongly judge their spiritual growth by emotions, circumstances, or religious activity. But true spiritual growth is not measured by how long you fast, how often you serve in church, or how passionately you worship during a service. These things can be helpful, but they are not the measuring rod. Motion is not the same as progress. You can be busy and still not be growing. You can be emotional and still not be spiritual. God does not look at your schedule or your religious performance. He looks at your spirit. That is why true growth can only be discerned spiritually, not carnally. Once you start using external metrics to assess your maturity, you fall into comparison, performance, pride, or discouragement. You begin to rate your growth against other people's appearances, rather than God's inward work in your life. The Galatian church made this same mistake. They started in the Spirit, embracing grace, walking by faith, depending on the finished work of Christ. But over time, they drifted. They turned to legalism, believing that they could perfect in the flesh what God had begun in the Spirit. Paul called this foolishness. Sadly, many Christians today make that same turn. But the way to grow spiritually is the same way you were saved by the Spirit, not by striving. Measure your growth not by your activity, but by your surrender. Not by your emotions, but by your increasing dependence on grace. Not by outward signs, but by the deepening of your walk in the Spirit. That is the only true measure of growth.

Quote of the Day: The way to grow spiritually is the same way you were saved: by the Spirit, not by striving.

PERSONAL RESPONSE:

1. Have you been using your church activity, emotions, or circumstances to judge how much you are growing spiritually?
2. Are you more focused on outward performance than on inward surrender to the Holy Spirit?
3. What changes do you need to make in how you measure your spiritual maturity?

Daily Prayer: Lord, I confess that I have often looked to the wrong things to measure my growth. Help me to stop chasing performance and start pursuing deeper surrender. Teach me to walk by the Spirit, depend on Your grace, and grow in quiet obedience. Let my life reflect the true marks of maturity, not busyness, but transformation. In Jesus' name, I pray. Amen.

Read the Bible in One Year: Job 5-7; Acts 8

OCTOBER 06

GIFTS VS GROWTH

> ***"Many will say to me in that day, Lord, Lord, have we not prophesied in thy name? and in thy name have cast out devils? and in thy name done many wonderful works? And then will I profess unto them, I never knew you: depart from me, ye that work iniquity."*** ***Matthew 7:22-23***

In today's Christian world, it is easy to confuse spiritual gifts with maturity. A man prophesies accurately, a woman prays in tongues for hours, or a young believer preaches powerfully, and we assume they are spiritually mature. But gifts are not proof of growth. They are manifestations of grace, not rewards for character.

1 Corinthians 12:7 says, *"But the manifestation of the Spirit is given to every man to profit withal."* Paul lists nine gifts in that chapter of scripture but none of them prove that a person is spiritually mature. Gifts are given; growth is cultivated. Gifts can build platforms; only fruit builds lives.

The Corinthian church flowed in spiritual gifts, yet Paul called them carnal. *"I... could not speak unto you as unto spiritual, but as unto carnal... babes in Christ"* (1 Corinthians 3:1). They were saved and gifted but immature. Jesus warned of this in our memory verse for today: many will say, "Lord, Lord," pointing to their gifts, but He will say, "I never knew you." The gifts were there, but the relationship was missing.

Charisma is not character. Samson had power but lacked discipline. Today, some build ministries while hiding addictions or pride. Do not measure growth by flash. Measure it by fruit. Ask yourself: Am I growing or just gifted?

Quote of the Day: Gifts are not proof of growth. They are manifestations of grace, not rewards for character.

PERSONAL RESPONSE

1. Have you confused spiritual gifts with spiritual maturity in your life or in how they assess others?
2. In what ways have you focused more on charisma, titles, or outward performance than on inward transformation?
3. What evidence of spiritual fruit can be seen in your daily walk?

Daily Prayer: Dear Lord, help me not to mistake my gifts for growth. Teach me to pursue fruit, not just flash. Expose every area of my heart where pride, immaturity, or performance has taken root. Grow me in the secret place until my life reflects Your Spirit in truth and character. In Jesus' name, I pray. Amen.

Read the Bible in One Year: Job 8-10

OCTOBER 07

MORAL CHANGES VS SPIRITUAL GROWTH

"Woe unto you, scribes and Pharisees, hypocrites! for ye are like unto whited sepulchres, which indeed appear beautiful outward, but are within full of dead men's bones, and of all uncleanness." Matthew 23:27

One of the greatest confusions among believers is assuming that moral improvement equals spiritual growth. You see someone who no longer lies, dresses modestly, or speaks respectfully, and conclude they are growing. But is that always true? Here is the hard truth: **moral change is not always spiritual growth.** Even unbelievers can be morally upright. A Muslim can be honest. An atheist can be kind. A traditionalist can show integrity. Morality, by itself, is not proof of spiritual transformation. It is possible to change outwardly and remain spiritually dead. Jesus rebuked this mindset harshly in our text. He was addressing people who looked clean but were unchanged at the core. That tells us that such a situation is very possible. Although **you cannot grow spiritually without your behaviour changing**, **you can change your behaviour without growing spiritually.** True transformation starts in the spirit and works outward. It is not about trimming the branches; it is about changing the root. Think of a morally upright atheist, disciplined and kind, yet spiritually lost. Contrast that with a struggling new believer, messy on the outside, but deeply yearning to please God. That longing, that heart-level shift, that is real growth. Do not confuse Christian behaviour with Christlike transformation. Many adapt to religious settings without letting the Spirit do real work. They act Christian but have not become Christlike. Ask yourself: *Is my growth deep or just decorative? Is the Spirit shaping my heart or am I maintaining an image?* **The Bible never says "be improved." It says,** *"Be ye transformed..."* **(Romans 12:2).** That is not surface polish; it is Spirit-powered change from within. Let God work on your roots. The fruit will follow.

Quote of the Day: Morality, by itself, is not proof of spiritual transformation. It is possible to change outwardly and remain spiritually dead.

PERSONAL RESPONSE:

1. Have you mistaken outward moral behaviour for true spiritual transformation in your own life?
2. Is your growth rooted in a deepening relationship with the Holy Spirit, or just in learning how to act Christian?
3. Are you allowing God to transform your heart, or are you merely adjusting your habits to fit into a religious environment?

Daily Prayer: Heavenly Father, I do not want a life that looks clean on the outside but remains untouched on the inside. I surrender my heart to You again today. Do the deep work in me that only Your Spirit can do. Help me not to settle for surface change but to pursue real transformation from within. Make me more like Jesus, from the inside out. In His name I pray, Amen.

Read the Bible in One Year: Job 11-13; Acts 9

OCTOBER 08

THE PATH OF TRUE GROWTH

"Keep thy heart with all diligence; for out of it are the issues of life." Proverbs 4:23

Spiritual growth always flows from the inside out. That is how God designed it. He begins His work in your spirit, and from there it spreads into your mind, habits, relationships, and lifestyle. But the order is crucial: it starts within.

The world teaches the opposite. From childhood, we were taught to grow from the outside in by observing, imitating, and conforming. Our progress was judged by how well we behaved or performed. Even now, society rewards appearances, possessions, and achievements. But God does not measure growth that way. His eyes are on the heart.

Our text says, *"Keep thy heart with all diligence; for out of it are the issues of life."* Everything in your life flows from your heart, your spirit. If the fountain is polluted, the water will be bitter. But if the source is pure, the fruit will be sweet. God transforms the fountain, not just the flow.

Religion works from the outside in by adjusting your behaviour. But God works from the inside out by renewing your mind, softening your heart, and changing your desires. True spiritual growth produces the fruit of the Spirit, not just public performance.

So ask yourself: *Am I changing at the root, or just at the surface?* Inside-out growth may not be flashy, but it is real and lasting.

Quote of the Day: Spiritual growth always flows from the inside out. That is how God designed it. He begins His work in your spirit, and from there it spreads into your mind, habits, relationships, and lifestyle.

PERSONAL RESPONSE:

1. Are you simply adjusting to Christian expectations, or is the Holy Spirit doing a real work in your heart?
2. Are you measuring your growth by outward change, or by the fruit of the Spirit developing within you?
3. Is your transformation flowing from a changed fountain, or are you just polishing the surface?

1. **Daily Prayer:** Father, I surrender my heart to You today. Work in me from the inside out. Do not let me settle for surface change or religious performance. Renew my mind. Transform my desires. Reorder my affections. In Jesus' name, I pray. Amen.

Read the Bible in One Year: Job 14-16

THE CORE EVIDENCE OF SPIRITUAL GROWTH

"But the fruit of the Spirit is love, joy, peace, longsuffering, gentleness, goodness, faith, meekness, temperance: against such there is no law." Galatians 5:22–23

If you want to assess your spiritual growth, do not look at your gifts, titles, or church activities, look at your fruit. Are you bearing the fruit of the Spirit as clearly defined in our text above? That is the real evidence of spiritual maturity.

It is called *fruit of the Spirit*, not *fruit of your effort*. You do not force or fake it; it grows naturally when you stay rooted in Christ. Just like a tree does not strain to bear fruit but draws life from its roots, you bear spiritual fruit by abiding in Jesus. Love begins to flow through you. Joy becomes deeper. Peace settles your soul. Patience, kindness, and self-control begin to define your actions. This is not perfection; it is direction. You may not be where you want to be, but you are no longer who you used to be. That is growth. Paul emphasizes this in 1 Corinthians 13: Even if you prophesy, speak in tongues, perform miracles, or give all your goods to the poor, without love, you are nothing. So do not confuse spiritual activity with spiritual maturity. You can lead, teach, or serve and still lack growth if your heart remains bitter, impatient, or proud. True growth happens when you abide in Christ (John 15:5). It is not about trying harder; it is about staying connected. Fruit is not produced by pressure but by presence. Ask yourself: *What is the Holy Spirit producing in me?* When fruit begins to grow, you are not just acting like a Christian; you are becoming like Christ.

Quote of the Day: When fruit begins to grow, you are not just acting like a Christian; you are becoming like Christ.

PERSONAL RESPONSE:

1. Are you more focused on developing your gifts than bearing the fruit of the Spirit?
2. Can the people closest to you testify that love, joy, peace, and patience are increasing in your life?
3. Are you staying connected to Christ daily so that your growth flows from His presence, not your performance?

Daily Prayer: Father, thank You for showing me that true spiritual growth is measured by fruit, not performance. Help me to stay rooted in Christ, drawing strength and character from Your Spirit each day. I do not want to fake maturity or settle for outward activity; I want to be transformed from within. Keep me abiding in You, Lord, so that what I do flows from who I am in You. Grow Your fruit in me. In Jesus' name, I pray. Amen.

Read the Bible in One Year: Job 17-19

WHAT REALLY GROWS WHEN YOU GROW SPIRITUALLY? Part 1

"God is a Spirit: and they that worship him must worship him in spirit and in truth." John 4:24

What exactly grows in spiritual growth? Many believers never pause to ask this question, and as a result, they spend years feeding and exercising the wrong thing. This confusion often leads to frustration and burnout in the Christian walk.

If you think spiritual growth means a stronger willpower, you will exhaust yourself trying to say "No" to sin. If you think it is about guilt and sin-consciousness, you will sink into self-condemnation whenever you fail. If you think it is about behaviour, your Christian life will become a checklist: dry, external, and joyless. These things are not evil, but they are not the core of growth. They are *fruit*, not *root*. Here is the truth: **In spiritual growth, you grow your spirit man.** Not your emotions, not your willpower, not your religious reputation, but your spirit man. That is the part of you born of God, recreated in Christ, and seated with Him in heavenly places. That is the real you, and that is where true growth must happen. Think of it like this: You can go on a crash diet and look slim but remain unhealthy. Or you can eat well, rest, and build strength and become truly healthy. The first way is faster, but it is fake. The same is true spiritually. The second way is slower, but it is real. Real growth happens in your spirit and from there, genuine transformation flows outward. So ask yourself: *What have I really been trying to grow?* It is time to unlearn false assumptions and refocus your walk with God on the right centre: your spirit man. When that part of you begins to grow, everything else will follow.

Quote of the Day: In spiritual growth, you grow your spirit man. Not your emotions, not your willpower, not your religious reputation, but your spirit man.

PERSONAL RESPONSE:

1. Have you been focusing more on growing your willpower, emotions, or behaviour instead of your spirit?
2. In what areas of your life have you measured growth by outward change rather than inward transformation?
3. Are you willing to unlearn wrong patterns and refocus your walk with God around growing your spirit man?

Daily Prayer: Lord, help me to stop chasing outward performance and start nurturing my spirit man. Teach me to grow from the inside out. I surrender my habits, emotions, and thoughts to You. Please align them with the life of Christ in me. Let my transformation be real, lasting, and led by Your Spirit. In Jesus' name, Amen.

Read the Bible in One Year: Job 20-21; Acts 10

OCTOBER 11

WHAT REALLY GROWS WHEN YOU GROW SPIRITUALLY? Part 2

"And the very God of peace sanctify you wholly; and I pray God your whole spirit and soul and body be preserved blameless unto the coming of our Lord Jesus Christ." 1 Thessalonians 5:23

Yesterday, we saw that what truly grows in spiritual growth is your *spirit man.* That truth is so vital, it bears repeating today.

The Bible distinguishes your **spirit, soul**, and **body**, as can be clearly seen in the text quoted above. Your **body** is the physical side of you. Your **soul** is the seat of thoughts, will, and emotions. But your **spirit** is the real you, your innermost being, the part that connects directly with God.

Jesus said, *"God is a Spirit: and they that worship him must worship him in spirit and in truth"* (John 4:24). This means spiritual growth is not about improving your emotions or polishing your habits. It is about nurturing your spirit man, the core of your being. Behavioural change may follow, but it is not the goal; it is the fruit.

Picture a tree: the **root** is your spirit man, the **trunk and branches** are your soul, and the **fruit** is your behaviour. If you focus only on fruit, neglecting the root, growth will be shallow and temporary. But when you feed your spirit with prayer, the Word, and the Holy Spirit's presence, change happens from within. Your actions shift because your nature is growing.

Do not settle for surface-level change. Tend the root. Grow your spirit man. That is where true, lasting transformation begins.

Quote of the Day: Spiritual growth is not about improving your emotions or polishing your habits. It is about nurturing your spirit man, the core of your being.

PERSONAL RESPONSE:

1. Are you focusing more on managing your outward behaviour than nurturing your inner spirit?
2. What practical steps are you taking daily to grow your spirit man through fellowship with God?
3. In what ways has your spiritual growth affected your thoughts, emotions, and actions recently?

Daily Prayer: Father, I thank You for giving me a new spirit when I came to Christ. Help me to grow my spirit man daily through Your Word, prayer, and communion with the Holy Spirit. Teach me to live from the inside out, that my life may reflect the transformation You are working in me. I do not want shallow change. I want true, lasting growth that begins in my spirit. In Jesus' name, amen.

Read the Bible in One Year: Job 22-24; Acts 11

STOP GROWING THE WRONG THING

"For what I am doing, I do not understand. For what I will to do, that I do not practice; but what I hate, that I do." Romans 7:15 (NKJV)

Meet Cynthia. She is sincere, loves God, reads her Bible, serves in church, but she is caught in a private war with pornography. She fasts, prays, joins accountability groups, and makes fresh commitments. Yet she keeps falling. Sound familiar?

Maybe your struggle is different, but the cycle feels the same: strong willpower, repeated failure, guilt, resolve, and relapse. Like Paul in our text above, you want to do what is right, but you keep doing what you hate. Why? Because willpower cannot defeat sin. Trying harder is not the answer. It never was.

Many believers, like Cynthia, are growing the wrong thing. They think that if they could just strengthen their will and be more focused or more self-controlled, they will finally win. But willpower cannot fix what is rooted deeper. As John Mark Comer puts it: "Willpower versus a second cookie is one thing… But willpower versus triggered trauma? Or willpower versus addiction? It doesn't stand a chance."

Romans 7 describes a believer still depending on the flesh instead of the Spirit. Paul asks, "Who shall deliver me?" and then answers: "I thank God through Jesus Christ our Lord" (Romans 7:24–25). Deliverance comes when you stop trying to fix your flesh and start feeding your spirit. That is where lasting growth and true victory begin. Stop growing the wrong thing. Grow your spirit man.

Quote of the Day: Willpower cannot defeat sin. Trying harder is not the answer. It never was.

PERSONAL RESPONSE:

1. Have you been relying on your willpower instead of the Holy Spirit to overcome recurring struggles?
2. In what areas of your life have you been growing the wrong thing?
3. Are you willing to surrender control and allow the Holy Spirit to deal with the deep roots rather than just trimming the branches?

Daily Prayer: Dear Lord, I repent for the times I have trusted in my own strength instead of leaning on Your Spirit. I ask You to reach into the deep places of my heart and bring true transformation. Help me to stop striving in the flesh and start growing in the Spirit. In Jesus' name, amen.

Read the Bible in One Year: Job 25-27; Acts 12

OCTOBER 13

HOW GOD RELATES WITH US

"The spirit of man is the candle of the Lord, searching all the inward parts of the belly." Proverbs 20:27

Spiritual growth is all about growing your spirit man, the innermost part of your being. But why is this so vital? Because God is Spirit (John 4:24), and He relates to you **spirit to spirit.** Your spirit is the primary channel through which God communicates, guides, and transforms you.

As you can see in our memory verse above, your spirit is like a lamp lit by the Lord, shining light into the deepest parts of your being. Just as ancient oil lamps required careful tending, your spirit must be nurtured to stay sensitive to God.

Romans 8:14 says, *"For as many as are led by the Spirit of God, they are the sons of God."* This means your spirit must be alive and growing to truly follow God's leading. As your spirit matures, you become more sensitive to His voice and more responsive to His promptings.

God does not primarily lead you through your mind or emotions. He leads you through your spirit. If your spirit is weak or neglected, you will struggle to discern His guidance. But when your spirit is strong, it acts like a finely tuned receiver, quick to detect divine signals, promptings, and insights.

Growing your spirit man increases your capacity for spiritual revelation, clarity in decision-making, and intimacy with God. Without this spirit-to-spirit connection, your faith becomes burdensome, and your efforts ineffective.

So ask yourself: How strong is my spirit man? If you want to walk closely with God and grow deeply in Him, you must prioritize your spirit because that is where God meets you.

Quote of the Day: If you want to walk closely with God and grow deeply in Him, you must prioritize your spirit because that is where God meets you.

PERSONAL RESPONSE:

1. How often do you intentionally feed and nurture your spirit man through prayer, Scripture, and fellowship with the Holy Spirit?
2. In what areas of your life do you tend to rely more on your emotions or logic than on your spirit?
3. How can you grow more sensitive to God's voice and promptings in your daily walk with Him?

Daily Prayer: Father, I thank You for creating me with a spirit that can commune with You. Help me to grow my spirit man every day so I can hear You clearly, follow You closely, and live in constant fellowship with You. Light the candle of my spirit with Your presence, and teach me to be led by Your Spirit in all things. In Jesus' name, Amen.

Read the Bible in One Year: Job 28-29; Acts 13

OCTOBER 14

WHY WILLPOWER CANNOT OVERCOME SIN

"For I know that in me (that is, in my flesh) nothing good dwells; for to will is present with me, but how to perform what is good I do not find. For the good that I will to do, I do not do; but the evil I will not to do, that I practice. Now if I do what I will not to do, it is no longer I who do it, but sin that dwells in me. I find then a law, that evil is present with me, the one who wills to do good." Romans 7:18–21 (NKJV)

In the text above, Paul confesses a struggle familiar to many. Paul wants to do right but finds himself constantly failing. His will is strong, but his performance is weak. Why? Because sin is not conquered by willpower; it is conquered by the Spirit.

This is the mistake many believers make. They think if they just try harder, fast more, or build stricter habits, they will overcome sin. But Paul says in **Galatians 5:17**:

"The flesh lusts against the Spirit... so that ye cannot do the things that ye would."

Desire is not the problem; power is. The flesh is like gravity: always pulling you downward. Willpower may get you off the ground briefly, but it cannot keep you flying. You need something stronger: the "law of the Spirit of life in Christ Jesus" (Romans 8:2). Willpower targets behaviour; the Spirit transforms nature. Willpower can open your Bible, but only the Spirit can make it alive in you. Willpower can say no to sin, but only the Spirit can break its power. You were never meant to overcome sin by self-effort. Your job is to grow your spirit and let the Spirit lead. Do not just try harder; train your spirit, sow to the Spirit, and abide in Christ. That is how real, lasting victory comes. You need more than a strong will. You need a strong spirit. And that comes only by walking in the Spirit.

Quote of the Day: Sin is not conquered by willpower; it is conquered by the Spirit.

PERSONAL RESPONSE

1. Are you trying to conquer sin through sheer willpower, or are you learning to rely on the Holy Spirit within you?
2. What are the areas in your life where your will keeps failing but your spirit has not yet been fed or strengthened?
3. How consistently are you sowing into your spirit through prayer, Scripture, and submission to the Spirit's leading?

Daily Prayer: Dear Lord, I confess that I have often tried to overcome sin by my own strength. I have relied on discipline and effort instead of leaning on Your Spirit. Please forgive me for trying to win spiritual battles in the flesh. Teach me how to grow my spirit and walk in step with You daily. In Jesus' name, Amen.

Read the Bible in One Year: Job 30-31

THE TRAP OF SIN-CONSCIOUSNESS

"What shall we say then? Is the law sin? Certainly not! On the contrary, I would not have known sin except through the law. For I would not have known covetousness unless the law had said, 'You shall not covet.' But sin, taking opportunity by the commandment, produced in me all manner of evil desire. For apart from the law sin was dead." Romans 7:7–8 (NKJV)

Yesterday we saw why willpower cannot overcome sin. Today, we will be looking at another trap many believers fall into on the path to spiritual growth: sin-consciousness. Sin-consciousness means you are constantly aware of your sin, dwelling on failures, replaying mistakes, and judging yourself harshly. While conviction by the Spirit brings repentance and growth, sin-consciousness traps you in guilt and shame. It becomes your identity. Your faith turns into performance, and you measure spirituality by how little you sin, not by how much you trust Christ. This is not God's design. The law brings awareness of sin but not the power to overcome it. Paul explains in *2 Corinthians 3:6*: *"The letter kills, but the Spirit gives life."*

As can be seen in today's text, the law magnifies sin-consciousness. It points you to your shortcomings, and the more your focus stays on your shortcomings, the more you spiral into self-condemnation instead of transformation. So how do you break free? Shift your focus. Ask yourself: *Am I sin-aware or Christ-aware?* To be Christ-aware is to fix your eyes on Jesus, knowing that His blood has already cleansed you. You still repent, but not from a place of shame. You grow by grace, not guilt; by the Spirit, not performance. *2 Corinthians 5:17* reminds us: *"If anyone is in Christ, he is a new creation; old things have passed away; behold, all things have become new."* You are not defined by past failures. You are renewed in Christ. True growth comes not by obsessing over sin, but by embracing your Spirit-led identity in Him.

Quote of the Day: You are not defined by past failures. You are renewed in Christ. True growth comes not by obsessing over sin, but by embracing your Spirit-led identity in Him.

PERSONAL RESPONSE:

1. Are you more aware of your sins and shortcomings than of Christ's righteousness and grace in your life?
2. Do you measure your spiritual growth by your performance, or by how much you are trusting and yielding to the Holy Spirit?
3. In moments of failure, do you run to God in faith or away from Him in guilt and self-condemnation?

Daily Prayer: Heavenly Father, I thank You that I am a new creature in Christ. I reject the lie of sin-consciousness and embrace the truth of my righteousness in You, in Jesus' name, Amen.

Read the Bible in One Year: Job 32-33; Acts 14

THE TRAP OF SELF-DRIVEN SPIRITUALITY

"I am the vine, you are the branches. He who abides in Me, and I in him, bears much fruit; for without Me you can do nothing." John 15:5

Self-effort in spiritual growth often looks noble, but beneath that struggle lies a subtle danger: the belief that *you* are responsible for transforming *yourself*. That belief is a trap.

When spiritual growth becomes self-managed, it turns into performance. You begin to measure your worth by how much you pray, how many chapters of the Bible you read, or how well you resist sin. When you succeed, you feel spiritual. When you fail, you feel condemned. Either way, the focus is on *you*, your effort, your strength, your scorecard.

This is how many sincere believers burn out. They start hungry for God, but after months of exhausting effort with little inward change, the fire dies. They keep the routine, but the joy is gone. Pretending replaces intimacy. Not out of rebellion, but out of weariness. Here is the truth: you were never meant to sanctify yourself. You cannot grow into Christlikeness by willpower. That is not how grace works. Spiritual disciplines like prayer, fasting, and Bible study are vital, but they are not the source of growth. They are tools, not trophies. They are meant to connect you to Christ, not replace Him. Jesus did not say, "Strive hard and bear fruit." He said, "Abide in Me... and you will bear much fruit". Growth is not a reward you earn; it is a fruit you bear by staying rooted in Christ. Your role is to abide. His role is to transform.

So if you feel weary and stuck, maybe it is time to stop striving harder and start trusting deeper. You were never meant to grow alone.

Quote of the Day: Growth is not a reward you earn; it is a fruit you bear by staying rooted in Christ. Your role is to abide. His role is to transform.

PERSONAL RESPONSE:

1. In what ways have **you measured your spiritual growth** based on effort rather than abiding in Christ?
2. Are **you using spiritual disciplines** as tools to connect with God or as yardsticks to prove your spirituality?
3. What would change in **your walk with God** if you focused less on performance and more on intimacy with Him?

Daily Prayer: Heavenly Father, I confess that I often try to grow by my own strength. I lay down my pride and striving, and I choose to trust You deeply. Teach me to abide in Christ, not just to perform for You. Let every discipline draw me closer, not make me feel condemned. I receive Your grace again today. Transform me from the inside out. Amen.

Read the Bible in One Year: Job 34-35; Acts 15

THE HOLY SPIRIT AS THE GROWER IN SPIRITUAL GROWTH

"But as it is written: 'Eye has not seen, nor ear heard, nor have entered into the heart of man the things which God has prepared for those who love Him. But God has revealed them to us through His Spirit. For the Spirit searches all things, yes, the deep things of God." 1 Corinthians 2:9-10

Let's be clear: you do not grow yourself. No matter how disciplined or desperate you may be, you can never be the source of your transformation. Only the Holy Spirit grows you. He is the Grower in spiritual growth. Your role is not to produce maturity but to yield to Him.

Jesus said, *"He shall teach you all things"* (John 14:26) and *"He will guide you into all truth"* (John 16:13). Paul affirms this in our text: *"God hath revealed [the deep things] unto us by His Spirit."* You do not access the deep things of God through intellect or effort. Only the Spirit can reveal them.

So where do spiritual disciplines like prayer, fasting and Bible study fit in? They are not growth mechanisms on their own. They do not transform you. They position you to stay yielded to the Spirit. Think of them as opening the blinds to let sunlight in. You do not create the light; you simply make room for it. That is why intimacy with the Holy Spirit is essential. Many believers have the Spirit but do not fellowship with Him. They live like spiritual singles, checking in only when needed. But the Holy Spirit was not sent just to be present; He was sent to be your Helper, Guide, and Teacher. You grow by remaining in fellowship, talking with Him, inviting Him into your thoughts, obeying His nudges, and listening to His voice. You do not grow by force but by fellowship. Let it sink in: You are not the gardener. The Spirit is. You are not the grower. You are the ground.

Quote of the Day: The Holy Spirit was not sent just to be present; He was sent to be your Helper, Guide, and Teacher.

PERSONAL RESPONSE

1. In what ways have you relied more on self-effort than on the Holy Spirit in your journey of spiritual growth?
2. What specific spiritual discipline in your life needs to shift from being a performance to becoming a place of fellowship with the Holy Spirit?
3. How can you become more intentional this week in inviting the Holy Spirit into your daily thoughts, decisions, and devotions?

Daily Prayer: Holy Spirit, I acknowledge that I cannot grow myself. Teach me to stop striving and start surrendering. Help me make room for You daily, not just through routines, but through real fellowship. Grow me from the inside out, and let my life bear fruit that brings glory to God. In Jesus' dear name, I pray. Amen.

Read the Bible in One Year: Job 36-37

WHY ONLY THE HOLY SPIRIT CAN GROW YOU

"For what man knoweth the things of a man, save the spirit of man which is in him? Even so the things of God knoweth no man, but the Spirit of God." 1 Corinthians 2:11

Only the Spirit of God knows the things of God. Without the Spirit, divine understanding is inaccessible. No matter how sincere you are, if the Spirit does not reveal it, you won't know it.

Imagine a dog trying to understand taxes or Shakespeare. It cannot! Now, imagine a flea trying to understand the heart of a dog. That is us, trying to understand God without His Spirit. The gap is too wide to be bridged by mere intellect and effort.

Isaiah 55:9 declares: *"For as the heavens are higher than the earth, so are my ways higher than your ways, and my thoughts than your thoughts."*

God's thoughts are not just different; they are infinitely higher. That is why spiritual growth is not humanly engineered; it is spiritually revealed. 1 Corinthians 2:10–12 says: *"But God hath revealed them unto us by his Spirit… that we might know the things that are freely given to us of God."*

The Spirit does not assist you; He authors your growth. Like a mountain guide, He knows the safest route, the needed pace, and the dangers to avoid. You grow, not because you try harder, but because you follow His lead.

So yield. Stop trying to manage your own maturity. Let the Holy Spirit take the lead. Only He knows what you truly need next. Only He can grow you.

Quote of the Day: Stop trying to manage your own maturity. Let the Holy Spirit take the lead. Only He knows what you truly need next. Only He can grow you.

PERSONAL RESPONSE:

1. In what areas of your spiritual life are you still relying on personal effort instead of depending on the Holy Spirit?
2. How has your understanding of spiritual growth changed after realizing that only the Holy Spirit knows the things of God?
3. What practical steps can you take this week to yield more intentionally to the Holy Spirit's guidance in your daily walk?

Daily Prayer: Holy Spirit, I confess that I often try to grow myself by my own strength. Today, I surrender. Teach me, guide me, and reveal to me the deep things of God. Lead me on the path of true transformation. I yield to Your wisdom, Your timing, and Your leadership. Amen.

Read the Bible in One Year: Job 38-40

OCTOBER 19

THE HOLY SPIRIT'S EXCLUSIVE ROLE IN REVELATION

"But the natural man receiveth not the things of the Spirit of God: for they are foolishness unto him: neither can he know them, because they are spiritually discerned." 1 Corinthians 2:14

Only the Holy Spirit can reveal God's heart to you; not your intellect, not your pastor, not your Bible study group. These are helpful, but they cannot replace the Spirit. Spiritual truth is not grasped by intellect; it is revealed by the Spirit. You can be surrounded by truth and still remain blind without Him.

The Holy Spirit does not just help you study the Bible; He makes it come alive. A passage you have read a hundred times can suddenly pierce your heart, not through explanation, but through revelation. Teachers explain; the Spirit transforms. Ever listened to a great sermon and walked away unchanged? You understood the words but remained the same. That is the difference between information and revelation: one touches your mind, the other touches your spirit. This is the crisis in many churches: we have substituted revelation with head knowledge. We have trained professional Christians fluent in Scripture but disconnected from the Spirit. The result? Religion without life. Jesus warned the Pharisees in John 5:39–40: *"Search the scriptures... and they are they which testify of me. And ye will not come to me, that ye might have life."* They knew the Word but missed the Person behind it. Teachers can give you the map, but only the Spirit takes you on the journey. As Paul said in 1 Corinthians 3:6–7, only God gives the increase. Seek the Spirit, not just more sermons. Invite Him to reveal, convict, and transform. Because without Him, we are just guessing.

Quote of the Day: Spiritual truth is not grasped by intellect; it is revealed by the Spirit. You can be surrounded by truth and still remain blind without Him.

PERSONAL RESPONSE QUESTIONS

1. How has your approach to spiritual growth relied more on intellectual study or human teaching than on the Holy Spirit's revelation?
2. Can you identify an area in your life where you have gained knowledge but lack transformation?
3. In what ways are you actively seeking intimacy with the Holy Spirit during Bible study, prayer, or worship?

Daily Prayer: Holy Spirit, I acknowledge that no true revelation comes apart from You. I yield my mind, heart, and spirit to Your light. Make the Word come alive in me. Open my eyes to see Christ, not just verses. Lead me beyond information into transformation, and let every moment in Scripture be an encounter with the Living God. In Jesus' dear name, I pray. Amen.

Read the Bible in One Year: Job 41-42; Acts 16

OCTOBER 20

FROM PERFORMANCE TO PARTNERSHIP

> ***"For as many as are led by the Spirit of God, they are the sons of God." Romans 8:14***

Many of us were raised to think that the Christian life is all about performance: pray more, read more, serve more, fast more. So we strive and set spiritual goals. When we succeed, we feel spiritual pride. When we fail, we feel shame or burnout. But performance-driven spirituality cannot produce true life. It leads to exhaustion, not transformation.

The gospel is not a call to strive harder; it is an invitation to surrender to the Holy Spirit. He is the Grower. He is the Power. He is the Life. Spiritual growth comes through **partnership,** not performance.

Look at the wordings of our text again. Paul did not say, "As many as pray the most" or "serve the most." He said those **led** by the Spirit, they are the sons of God.

This life of surrender is not passive or lazy; it is **active cooperation.** You show up, you listen, you obey, and the Spirit transforms you in ways your effort never could. Think of it like dancing: the Spirit leads, you follow. Or like sailing: you cannot make the wind blow, but you can raise your sail. That is what spiritual disciplines do. They position you to catch the wind of the Spirit.

So shift your mindset. Let go of the guilt-driven hustle and embrace the Spirit's leadership. Talk to Him. Trust Him. Follow Him. Rest in the truth that you are not growing alone.

The Christian life is not a solo performance, it is a sacred partnership. And the Holy Spirit is reaching for your hand. Will you take it?

Quote of the Day: The gospel is not a call to strive harder; it is an invitation to surrender to the Holy Spirit.

PERSONAL RESPONSE:

1. In what areas of your spiritual life have you unknowingly slipped into a performance mindset rather than a partnership with the Holy Spirit?
2. How does understanding that the Holy Spirit leads, rather than your effort, reshape the way you approach spiritual disciplines?
3. What practical steps can you take this week to shift from striving in your strength to surrendering to the Spirit's guidance?

Daily Prayer: Holy Spirit, I confess that I often try to grow myself through effort and striving. Today, I surrender my need to perform and ask You to lead me. Teach me to follow You, trust Your timing, and rest in Your power. Help me to grow not by pressure, but by partnership with You. In Jesus' name, Amen.

Read the Bible in One Year: Psalms 1-3; Acts 17

HE WILL GUIDE YOU INTO ALL TRUTH

"Howbeit when he, the Spirit of truth, is come, he will guide you into all truth: for he shall not speak of himself; but whatsoever he shall hear, that shall he speak: and he will shew you things to come." John 16:13

One of Jesus' most comforting promises about the Holy Spirit is in the verse quoted above. Notice that word **guide**. The Spirit does not drop all truth on you at once; He leads you into it progressively. Why? Because you cannot handle everything now. That's exactly what Jesus said in John 16:12:

"I have yet many things to say unto you, but ye cannot bear them now."

Spiritual growth is not instant. It is a guided journey. Like a loving parent feeding a child, the Holy Spirit gives you truth in portions that fit your maturity. He is not a dump truck of knowledge, but a wise, intentional Teacher.

This should free you from pressure. You do not need to fake maturity or panic over what you do not yet understand. The Spirit is not frustrated with your pace. He is not comparing you to someone else. He knows where you are and where you are headed.

Think about it: some Scriptures that once seemed empty now come alive. Some convictions you carry today were not even on your radar last year. That is not coincidence. That is the Spirit guiding you, layer by layer, into deeper truth.

So do not rush. Do not compare. Do not despair. You are not behind. You are on schedule. The Holy Spirit is your personal Guide, and He is taking you exactly where God wants you, step by step, truth by truth. Trust Him. He is faithful to finish what He started.

Quote of the Day: Spiritual growth is not instant. It is a guided journey. Like a loving parent feeding a child, the Holy Spirit gives you truth in portions that fit your maturity.

PERSONAL RESPONSE:

1. Are you impatient with the pace of your spiritual growth, or have you learned to trust the Holy Spirit's process in your life?
2. In what ways has the Holy Spirit gradually revealed truth to you that you were not ready for in an earlier season?
3. What specific step can you take today to stay in step with the Spirit rather than striving to figure things out on your own?

Daily Prayer: Holy Spirit, thank You for being my patient and wise Guide. Help me to stop striving and start trusting. Teach me to rest in Your timing, stay sensitive to Your voice, and yield fully to Your leadership. I surrender to the process by which You are forming Christ in me. Amen.

Read the Bible in One Year: Psalms 4-6

TWO GOVERNMENTS

"For they that are after the flesh do mind the things of the flesh; but they that are after the Spirit the things of the Spirit. For to be carnally minded is death; but to be spiritually minded is life and peace. Because the carnal mind is enmity against God: for it is not subject to the law of God, neither indeed can be. So then they that are in the flesh cannot please God." Romans 8:5–8

The passage quoted above draws a sharp contrast between two ways of living: the government of the flesh and the government of the Spirit. These are not just tendencies or moods; they are ruling systems that shape how you think, desire, and live.

Paul writes, *"They that are after the flesh do mind the things of the flesh."* When governed by the flesh, your mindset revolves around self. Even spiritual habits may be motivated by self-interest. The flesh says, "I'll obey if it makes sense," or "I can handle this myself." It does not just ignore God; it opposes Him. *"The carnal mind is enmity against God... neither indeed can be."* The flesh can fake holiness, but it cannot produce true obedience.

But those who are governed by the Spirit *"mind the things of the Spirit."* Their desires shift. They love the Word, hunger for Jesus, and are quick to repent. They long for transformation, not just improvement. They value what the Spirit values. This is not behaviour modification; it is a new way of living.

Paul leaves no middle ground: *"To be carnally minded is death; but to be spiritually minded is life and peace."* The flesh kills intimacy, hunger, and clarity. The Spirit brings peace, vitality, and communion with God.

So here is the truth: you are always aligning with one of these governments. There is no neutral zone. Are your choices shaped by what feels good, or by what the Spirit is saying? Only one path leads to life. Choose your government, and choose it daily.

Quote of the Day: Are your choices shaped by what feels good, or by what the Spirit is saying? Only one path leads to life. Choose your government, and choose it daily.

PERSONAL RESPONSE:

1. Which mindset do you find yourself operating from more often, and how is it affecting your walk with God?
2. What are some signs in your life that indicate the flesh is still subtly in control, even in spiritual activities?
3. What practical steps can you take this week to intentionally shift the government of your life from the flesh to the Spirit?

Daily Prayer: Holy Spirit, I acknowledge that I cannot please God in the flesh. I surrender to Your government over my life. *In Jesus' name, Amen.*

Read the Bible in One Year: Psalms 10-12

THE HOLY SPIRIT IN YOU: RESIDENT OR PRESIDENT?

"If we live in the Spirit, let us also walk in the Spirit." Galatians 5:25

There is a difference between having the Holy Spirit **resident** in your life and having Him as **President.** Many believers stop at salvation. The Spirit lives in them, but He does not lead them. He is present, but not presiding.

Romans 8:9 says, *"Now if any man have not the Spirit of Christ, he is none of his."* So if you belong to Christ, the Holy Spirit is in you. But is He in charge?

Picture your life as a house. When you got saved, the Holy Spirit moved in. But in many lives, He is confined to the guest room. They still run the house, make the decisions, follow their impulses. The Spirit is present, but not President. He was never meant to be a silent guest. He came to govern your life. He does not just comfort you after a crash; He wants to drive so you avoid the crash. But here is the sobering truth: He will not force His way. He waits for your surrender. Galatians 5:16–17 says: *"Walk in the Spirit, and ye shall not fulfil the lust of the flesh... These are contrary... so that ye cannot do the things that ye would."*

There is a war inside you between the Spirit and the flesh. And until you yield, you remain stuck in spiritual tug-of-war. You cannot walk in the Spirit and still walk in self. The Holy Spirit wants more than permission to stay; He wants the keys. Growth, power, and victory come when you stop asking Him to assist your plans and start following His. So ask yourself: **Is the Holy Spirit merely resident in my life, or is He truly President?** Let Him lead. Give Him every room. That is where transformation begins.

Quote of the Day: The Holy Spirit wants more than permission to stay; He wants the keys.

PERSONAL RESPONSE:

1. If your life were a house, which areas have you fully surrendered to the Holy Spirit, and which areas are still under your control?
2. In what ways do you recognize the conflict between your flesh and the Spirit in your daily decisions?
3. How do you currently invite the Holy Spirit's leadership into your routine choices, priorities, and goals?

Daily Prayer: Holy Spirit, I surrender. I do not want You to be a silent guest in my life; I want You to take full leadership. I give You every room, every key, every decision. Teach me to walk in step with You daily. Expose the places where I still try to stay in control, and help me yield fully to Your rule. Be not just resident in me, but President over me. In Jesus' name, Amen.

Read the Bible in One Year: Psalms 13-15; Acts 19

OCTOBER 24

THE CORINTHIAN PROBLEM

"And I, brethren, could not speak unto you as unto spiritual, but as unto carnal, even as unto babes in Christ." 1 Corinthians 3:1

The Corinthian church is a sobering example of believers who were saved, gifted, and yet spiritually immature. They had received the gospel, were filled with the Holy Spirit, and operated in spiritual gifts, yet Paul still called them *carnal.* He did not question their salvation but confronted their lack of growth. In **1 Corinthians 3:1–3**, Paul calls them *babes in Christ*, not ready for solid food, still ruled by envy, strife, and division. They walked "as men". That is, like people without the Spirit. The Spirit was present, but not president. First, they were divided. They formed cliques around Paul, Apollos, and others (1 Corinthians 1:12), turning church into a popularity contest. Second, they tolerated gross immorality (1 Corinthians 5:1), even celebrating what should have brought them to their knees in repentance. Third, they were spiritually immature: rich in gifts but poor in fruit. They used their gifts to show off, not to edify. That is why Paul wrote 1 Corinthians 13, not for weddings, but as a rebuke. *"Though I speak with the tongues of men and of angels, and have not charity, I am become as sounding brass..."* (v.1). True spirituality is not defined by gifts, but by love which only the Spirit produces. The Corinthian problem is still with us today: activity without maturity, power without purity, charisma without character. So here is the question: Do you see any of Corinth in you? Are you Spirit-filled but self-led? Gifted but lacking fruit? The answer is not more activity, but deeper surrender. The Spirit won't force His way in. He waits to govern. And when He does, He brings transformation from carnal chaos to Christ-like character.

Who is in charge of your life?

Quote of the Day: True spirituality is not defined by gifts, but by love which only the Spirit produces.

PERSONAL RESPONSE:

1. In what ways do you see the "Corinthian condition" showing up in your own life?
2. Are you more focused on spiritual gifts and activities than on growing in your walk with God?
3. Is there any area in your life where the Holy Spirit has been prompting you to surrender, but you have been resisting?

Daily Prayer: Holy Spirit, I acknowledge that I have often settled for surface-level spirituality: gifts without fruit, activity without love, salvation without surrender. Please forgive me. I yield to Your rule today. Govern my thoughts, my choices, and my desires. Grow me out of childishness and carnality into the fullness of Christ. Teach me to walk in love, to pursue maturity, and to reflect Your character in all things. Amen.

Read the Bible in One Year: Psalms 16-17; Acts 20

THE ONLY PATH TO TRUE CHANGE

"Not by might, nor by power, but by my spirit, saith the Lord of hosts." Zechariah 4:6

No real transformation happens without the Holy Spirit. You may try to change yourself through rules, conferences, or powerful teaching, but unless the Spirit governs your life, any change will be shallow and short-lived.

Look at what God is saying in our memory verse above. That is not a slogan; it is a warning. Willpower cannot defeat the flesh. Discipline alone cannot conquer sin. Emotion may stir you, but only the Spirit can truly transform you.

Who is producing your growth? Your pastor? Your resolve? Your church programme? If it is not the Spirit, your growth will collapse under pressure. Only the Spirit can reach deep enough to change you from the inside out.

Yes, pastors and churches matter. God uses them to equip you. But, as Paul says in 1 Corinthians 3:6, *"I have planted, Apollos watered; but God gave the increase."* Only the Spirit gives growth. Your part is surrender.

Many believers are addicted to inputs like more sermons, books and events, hoping that one of them will finally trigger lasting change. But change does not come from accumulation. It comes from yielding. You grow when you let the Holy Spirit take over.

Galatians 5:16–17 says, *"Walk in the Spirit, and ye shall not fulfil the lust of the flesh…"* The way to overcome the flesh is not by fighting harder, but by walking in the Spirit. If you are stuck, the issue may not be sincerity; it may be surrender. The Spirit must not just be resident; He must be President. Stop striving. Start yielding. The Spirit-governed life is not optional. It is the only path to real, lasting change.

Quote of the Day: Only the Spirit gives growth. Your part is surrender.

PERSONAL RESPONSE:

1. In what areas of your life are you still relying on your own strength instead of the Holy Spirit's power?
2. Are there habits or struggles that have persisted despite your best efforts? What might surrendering those to the Spirit look like?
3. How can you practically shift from striving for change to yielding to the Spirit's leadership each day?

Daily Prayer: Holy Spirit, I acknowledge that I cannot truly change without You. Forgive me for trying to grow by my own strength. Today, I surrender afresh. Govern my heart, shape my desires, and produce in me the lasting fruit that only You can give. I yield to Your leadership. Take over completely. Amen.

Read the Bible in One Year: Psalms 18-19

OCTOBER 26

THE EXTRAORDINARY LIFE OF THE SPIRIT-GOVERNED BELIEVER

"The wind bloweth where it listeth, and thou hearest the sound thereof but canst not tell whence it cometh, and whither it goeth: so is every one that is born of the Spirit." John 3:8

This verse is talking about your identity as a child of God. You are born of the Spirit, and just like the wind, your life, when governed by the Spirit, will be mysterious, dynamic, and powerful. People may see your fruit but won't be able to explain your steps. You will not be bound by patterns, moods, or fleshly impulses. You will be led moment by moment by the Holy Spirit.

This is not a fantasy; it is your inheritance. The Spirit-governed life is not driven by offence, ambition, or fear. It is driven by revelation. You no longer react like others because you see beyond the natural.

Jesus modelled this. He said, *"The Son can do nothing of himself, but what he seeth the Father do…"* **John 5:19**. Every word He spoke and step He took was Spirit-led. He walked in a rhythm no one else understood; but Heaven did.

Stephen, though not an apostle, was so full of the Spirit that his enemies could not resist the wisdom he spoke (Acts 6:10). Paul, once a persecutor, lived by a new principle: **"Christ liveth in me..." (Galatians 2:20).** That is what it means to live an extraordinary life. Not because you are impressive, but because the Spirit of God is in charge.

Let the wind blow. Let the Spirit lead. Do not settle for ordinary. You were born of the Spirit to live a life that baffles the world and glorifies God.

Quote of the Day: You were born of the Spirit to live a life that baffles the world and glorifies God.

PERSONAL RESPONSE:

1. Would you describe your Christian life as ordinary or extraordinary? What makes you say so?
2. In what areas of your life are you still relying on logic, reputation, or routine instead of the Holy Spirit's leading?
3. When last did you respond to the Spirit's prompting in a way that defied natural reasoning but brought peace or fruit?

Daily Prayer: Holy Spirit, I surrender to Your leadership. I no longer want to live a life that is explainable only by human standards. Govern my thoughts, my steps, and my decisions. Let my life reflect the mystery, power, and freedom of one truly born of the Spirit. Lead me in a way that glorifies Jesus and makes Heaven proud. Amen.

Read the Bible in One Year: Psalms 20-22

FAITHFUL SERVICE: THE QUIET PROOF OF GROWTH

"But the fruit of the Spirit is love, joy, peace, longsuffering, kindness, goodness, faithfulness, gentleness, self-control. Against such there is no law." Galatians 5:22–23

In our devotional on the 9th of this month, we saw that the clearest sign of spiritual growth is the fruit of the Spirit. Galatians 5:22–23 lists them, and right there in the middle is one that is often overlooked but deeply vital: **faithfulness.** Faithfulness speaks of reliability, consistency, and loyalty, especially toward God. It is not loud or flashy, but it is powerful. You may not always feel spiritual "highs," but if you are walking faithfully, showing up, staying steady, and obeying God daily, you are growing. Spiritual growth is often quiet. It is seen in obedience when no one is watching. It is in doing what God called you to do, not for applause, but because He asked. That is maturity. Many mistake emotional experience for spiritual growth. But weeping in prayer or shaking in worship does not prove growth. The real test is what happens when the emotion fades: Are you still standing? Still serving? Still obeying?

Faithful service is not just a result of growth; it is a **proof** of it. One way to test your maturity is to check your record of service. Are you dependable? Can God trust you with responsibility without fear that you will abandon it? Do you serve without murmuring, even when no one sees?

In the end, what God rewards is not giftedness or hype. It is faithfulness. So keep showing up. Keep doing what He told you. Growth is not always dramatic but it is always dependable.

Quote of the Day: In the end, what God rewards is not giftedness or hype. It is faithfulness.

PERSONAL RESPONSE:

1. Would God describe you as faithful in the assignment He has committed to your hands?
2. Are there areas of your life where you have allowed emotions, or the lack of them, to dictate your consistency in walking with God?
3. Can others count on you to show up and serve, even when it is inconvenient or unnoticed?

Daily Prayer: Dear Lord, I may not always feel strong or spiritual, but today I ask You to make me faithful. Teach me to value steady obedience over emotional highs. Help me to keep showing up, to stay loyal to You, and to carry out my assignment without murmuring or seeking applause. May my life bear the quiet, enduring fruit of faithfulness. In Jesus' name, Amen.

Read the Bible in One Year: Psalms 23-25; Acts 21

A CALL TO STEWARDSHIP

"Well done, thou good and faithful servant: thou hast been faithful over a few things, I will make thee ruler over many." Matthew 25:21

In Matthew 25:14–30, Jesus tells a story of a master who entrusts his goods to three servants before traveling. One receives five talents, another two, and the last one, just one. Each according to their ability. Two servants invest and multiply what they are given. But the third buries his and returns it unused.

The master praises the first two. But to the third servant, he says: *"Thou wicked and slothful servant."* His talent is taken, and he is cast out. The message is clear: God expects fruitfulness. You are not here to hold space; you are here to steward something. Whether it is your gifts, time, opportunities, or story, God gave them for a purpose. You may not have five talents, but you have something. And you will give account. This parable reveals that promotion in God's kingdom is tied to faithfulness. Not fame. Not comparison. The one with two talents got the same reward as the one with five, because both were faithful. And this is not just about usefulness now; it is about eternity. One day, the Master will return. And you will not be judged by how much you had, but by how you used what you were given.

Faithfulness is not about impressing God; it is about responding to His trust. You do not need to be spectacular. You just need to be consistent. So ask yourself: Am I faithfully stewarding what God gave me? Or am I burying it out of fear or neglect? One day, Jesus will return. May you be found faithful. May you hear, "Well done."

Quote of the Day: Promotion in God's kingdom is tied to faithfulness.

PERSONAL RESPONSE:

1. Are you actively using the gifts, opportunities, and influence God has entrusted to you, or are you leaving them dormant out of fear, comparison, or complacency?
2. In what ways can you begin to treat your daily routines as opportunities for kingdom stewardship?
3. Would God describe your service as faithful? Can others consistently count on you to carry responsibility without murmuring or excuses?

Daily Prayer: Father, thank You for trusting me with gifts, opportunities, and responsibilities in Your kingdom. I confess that I have not always been faithful with what You have given. Today, I surrender afresh. Help me to be a faithful steward, diligent in little, consistent in much, and obedient in all. When You return, may I be found working, serving, and multiplying what You placed in my hands. Let me hear You say, "Well done." In Jesus' name, Amen.

Read the Bible in One Year: Psalms 26-28; Acts 22

ETERNITY-CONSCIOUSNESS VS EARTH-BOUND LIVING

"We look not at the things which are seen, but at the things which are not seen: for the things which are seen are temporal; but the things which are not seen are eternal." 2 Corinthians 4:18

One major obstacle to faithful service and true spiritual growth is earth-bound thinking. Many believers chase visibility, comfort, and applause, forgetting that we were saved not just from hell, but for purpose. You were born again to live with eternity in view.

The danger of earthward thinking is that it distorts your view of success. You start comparing gifts, measuring progress by numbers, and getting discouraged when unseen faithfulness seems unrewarded. But heaven has a different value system. God's reward is based on **faithfulness**, not visibility.

When you are eternity-conscious, you do not see delay as denial or obscurity as failure. You know that God is watching and preparing a reward. Yes, Christians will face judgment, not for sin, but for stewardship. At the **Judgment Seat of Christ (Bema)**, your works will be tested by fire. As **1 Corinthians 3:13–14** says, *"Every man's work shall be made manifest… the fire shall try every man's work… If any man's work abide… he shall receive a reward."*

That fire won't test your intentions; it will test your output. So ask yourself: **Am I living now in a way that will matter then?** Are you choosing faithfulness over convenience, service over self, and obedience over applause? Every unseen act of love builds something eternal. You are not just spending your life; you are investing it. Live for *that* day.

Let eternity shape your priorities, and you will find strength to serve faithfully, even when no one sees.

Quote of the Day: You were born again to live with eternity in view.

PERSONAL RESPONSE:

1. **What drives your decisions and priorities today?**
2. **Are there areas in your life where you have grown weary or careless in service because no one noticed or applauded? What would change if you truly believed God is watching and rewarding faithfulness?**
3. **If your life were tested by fire today, what part of your work would remain? What steps can you take to build with gold, silver, and precious stones instead of wood, hay, and stubble?**

Daily Prayer: Father, set my heart on eternal things. Deliver me from earth-bound thinking and help me live every day with the Judgment Seat of Christ in view. Teach me to serve faithfully, even in secret, knowing that You see, You remember, and You reward. In Jesus' name, Amen.

Read the Bible in One Year: Psalms 29-30; Acts 23

OCTOBER 30

HOW FAITHFUL SERVICE REVEALS SPIRITUAL GROWTH

"The Son of man came not to be ministered unto, but to minister, and to give his life a ransom for many." Matthew 20:28

Servanthood is the posture of one truly discipled by Christ. You cannot grow to be like Jesus and bypass the path of servanthood. He washed His disciples' feet. He chose the towel over the throne. He laid aside His garments, not because He lacked identity, but because He was secure in it.

To be a servant is to find joy in fulfilling another's will, especially God's. It is to love your Master enough to carry out His assignment, even if no one sees or applauds. Eleazar, Abraham's servant in Genesis 24, is a perfect picture. Entrusted with finding a wife for Isaac, he obeyed without hesitation. He bowed, prayed, listened, obeyed, and worshipped when God answered. He did not seek credit. He simply returned with results. That is maturity.

But servanthood is not always neat. Sometimes, it is forged in adversity. Look at Joseph: betrayed, enslaved, falsely accused, forgotten, yet always faithful. Whether in Potiphar's house or in prison, he served diligently. Genesis 39:3 says: *"His master saw that the Lord was with him... and made all that he did to prosper."* Joseph did not just go through trials; he grew through them. That is the mark of maturity: serving with integrity in hard seasons, stewarding what belongs to others even while waiting for your own promise. Can you serve when unrecognized? Can you stay joyful when overlooked? That is growth. God sees. He weighs your response in obscurity and lifts you at the right time. Faithful service is not just a duty; it is proof that you are becoming more like Jesus.

Quote of the Day: Faithful service is not just a duty; it is proof that you are becoming more like Jesus.

PERSONAL RESPONSE:

1. In what areas of life is God calling you to serve faithfully, even when no one is watching?
2. Have you ever been tempted to give up on serving because of lack of recognition or reward? How did you respond, and what would faithfulness look like instead?
3. Can God trust you to steward someone else's assignment with excellence while your own dream is still on hold?

Daily Prayer: Heavenly Father, shape my heart to reflect the servanthood of Jesus. Help me to serve with joy, obedience, and consistency, even in hidden or difficult seasons. May my life reveal true spiritual growth, not by position or applause, but by my faithfulness to You. In Jesus' name, Amen.

Read the Bible in One Year: Psalms 31-32

HOW THE HOLY SPIRIT EMPOWERS FAITHFUL SERVICE

"But the fruit of the Spirit is love, joy, peace, longsuffering, kindness, goodness, faithfulness, gentleness, self-control. Against such there is no law." Galatians 5:22–23

Galatians 5:22–23 lists **faithfulness** as an element of the fruit of the Spirit. That means you cannot serve God faithfully apart from a relationship with the Holy Spirit. Your consistency, integrity, and quiet perseverance in service cannot be sustained by willpower alone; it must flow from within.

There is a difference between self-driven service and Spirit-led service. Self-driven service often starts loud, fed by ego or the desire for applause. But when recognition fades, so does the motivation. Spirit-led service, however, is rooted and sustained. You keep showing up even when unnoticed. Why? Because the Spirit in you is faithful. Jesus said in John 15:5, *"I am the vine, ye are the branches… for without me ye can do nothing."* Faithful service flows from abiding in Christ. You cannot grow spiritually without the Spirit, and you cannot serve faithfully if you are not growing. The Holy Spirit strengthens your heart, deepens your convictions, and fills you with divine joy, even when service is tough or unrecognized. Stephen in Acts 6 is a powerful example. Though he was chosen to serve tables, he was described as **"full of the Holy Ghost and wisdom."** Serving behind the scenes still required spiritual depth. Paul also said, *"I laboured more abundantly… yet not I, but the grace of God which was with me."* (1 Corinthians 15:10). That grace flows through the Spirit. If you want to serve faithfully, stay rooted in fellowship with Him. You do not serve in your own strength. The One who called you is the One who empowers you. Let the Spirit grow you from the inside out.

Quote of the Day: If you want to serve faithfully, stay rooted in fellowship with the Holy Spirit.

PERSONAL RESPONSE:

1. In what areas of your life have you been relying more on self-effort than on the Holy Spirit's empowerment?
2. How can you deepen your daily fellowship with the Holy Spirit so that your service flows from intimacy rather than obligation?
3. Are there signs in your life that your service is rooted in fruitfulness rather than performance?

Daily Prayer: Holy Spirit, I surrender afresh to Your work in my heart. Grow the fruit of faithfulness in me and empower me to serve with joy, integrity, and consistency, even when no one sees but You. Let my service be rooted in intimacy, not effort. Make me a faithful branch that abides in Christ and bears lasting fruit. Amen.

Read the Bible in One Year: Psalms 33-34; Acts 24

NOVEMBER

WELCOME TO THE MONTH OF SERVANTHOOD

PROPHETIC DECREE

I decree that this month you are being redefined for Kingdom greatness through the spirit of servanthood. Every trace of pride, self-promotion, and worldly ambition is replaced with the humility and strength of Christ, the Servant King. You will walk the narrow road of true greatness, measured not by titles or applause, but by how deeply you serve and follow Jesus. The Holy Spirit will awaken in you a passion to live, lead, and labour like Christ. You will carry the anointing that rests on the lowly, with favour following you as you choose the towel over the throne. Each day will bring revelation, transformation, and a renewed longing to serve, as God entrusts you with divine assignments and eternal impact.

SERVANTHOOD

Welcome to a transformational journey into the heart of Kingdom greatness. This month's devotional is a call to servanthood. In a world obsessed with influence, visibility, and self-advancement, *servanthood* brings us back to the narrow road that Jesus Himself walked.

The spirit of this devotional is simple: to redefine greatness through the lens of service. In God's Kingdom, power flows through towels, not titles. Anointing rests on the lowly, not the lofty. And eternal impact is measured not by how many follow you, but by how faithfully you follow Christ.

Throughout this month, you will encounter truths that challenge the culture of self and awaken a deeper longing to live, lead, and labour like Jesus, the Servant King. Each day offers a focused meditation, Scripture-based insights, probing response questions, and a heartfelt prayer designed not just to inform you but to form Christ in you. Whether you are a pastor or a professional, a student or a leader, God is calling you to embody the kind of servant-heart that attracts His favour and power.

So pause. Breathe. Lay down your ambitions at the foot of the cross. And let your journey through this devotional recalibrate your soul for the only kind of greatness that counts in eternity: the greatness of a servant.

Let the journey begin!

TABLE OF CONTENTS

THE FIRST OFFERING GOD WANTS

"I beseech you therefore, brethren, by the mercies of God, that ye present your bodies a living sacrifice, holy, acceptable unto God, which is your reasonable service." Romans 12:1

When most people think of "serving God," they picture doing something like preaching, singing, giving, or volunteering. These are good, but is service really about what you do for God?

The world equates value with productivity. If you are not doing something visible, it feels like you are doing nothing valuable. But God sees things differently. While the world looks at your actions, God looks at your heart. He is not impressed by how much you *do* if you have not first given Him yourself.

In God's Kingdom, service begins with surrender. Before ministry, there must be offering. Not the offering of your gifts, talents, or time, but the offering of yourself. The first act of true service is not using your gift; it is presenting your life.

You can serve in every department of your church, go on mission trips, and still miss the point if you have never fully surrendered yourself to God. Until you give Him your heart, nothing you offer counts for eternity. God does not want your gifts apart from you. If He does not have the altar, He does not want the sacrifice.

This kind of surrender is not automatic. It is not inherited. It is a conscious decision. Without it, your service is shallow. With it, your smallest act becomes sacred.

So before you move on, pause and ask: *Have I truly given myself to God?* Because that is where service really begins.

Quote of the Day: In God's Kingdom, service begins with surrender.

PERSONAL RESPONSE:

1. Have you truly given yourself to God, or have you only been giving Him your gifts and activities?
2. What areas of your life are still on your terms instead of on God's altar?
3. If God asked for *you* today, not just what you can do, would He find a willing, surrendered heart?

Daily Prayer: Dear Lord, I offer myself to You, fully and without reservation. Help me to surrender my will, my desires, and my identity completely. Strip away every false offering, and take all of me. In Jesus' name, amen.

Read the Bible in One Year: Psalms 35-36; Acts 25

NOVEMBER 02

A LIVING SACRIFICE

"I beseech you therefore, brethren, by the mercies of God, that ye present your bodies a living sacrifice, holy, acceptable unto God, which is your reasonable service." Romans 12:1

In this verse, Paul makes a profound plea that captures the essence of what we learnt in yesterday's devotional. He uses the word *beseech*, showing that he is not commanding you. He is not forcing you. He is simply appealing to you, based on the mercy you have received. And what is he asking? That you present yourself to God as a *living sacrifice.*

To Paul's Roman audience, sacrifice meant one thing: death. Whether at the Jewish temple or pagan altars, sacrifice was total. An animal was slain, drained of blood, and consumed by fire. It was irreversible. So when Paul spoke of a *living* sacrifice, it sounded shocking. A sacrifice that stays alive? Still breathing after the altar? Yes. That is exactly what God wants.

To be a living sacrifice means your surrender is complete, but your life continues. You do not die physically, but you die to self. You give all of your will, your ambitions, and your rights to God. Every day, you choose to live, not for yourself, but for Him. This is not a one-time offering; it is daily, personal, and often unseen. But God sees. And He treasures it more than public achievements.

A living sacrifice is the kind of God wants. Not a dead gift, but a living you, fully surrendered, alive to His will, every day.

Quote of the Day: A living sacrifice is the kind of God wants. Not a dead gift, but a living you, fully surrendered, alive to His will, every day.

PERSONAL RESPONSE:

1. In what practical ways are you daily offering yourself as a living sacrifice to God?
2. What parts of your will or desires are still resisting full surrender to God's ownership?
3. Are you living each day for God's will or still making decisions centred around yourself?

Daily Prayer: Lord, I surrender my will to You today. Take all of me. Teach me to live each moment as a living sacrifice, wholly given to You, and fully alive to Your purpose for my life. In Jesus' name, amen.

Read the Bible in One Year: Psalms 37-39; Acts 26

YOUR REASONABLE SERVICE

"I beseech you therefore, brethren, by the mercies of God, that ye present your bodies a living sacrifice, holy, acceptable unto God, which is your reasonable service." Romans 12:1

When Paul urges you to present your body as a living sacrifice, he calls it your *reasonable* service. The word comes from the Greek *logikos* from which we get *logical*. Paul is not appealing to your emotions. He is saying: in light of God's mercy, surrendering your life to Him is the most logical thing you could do.

God is not asking for blind devotion. He is asking for a thoughtful, deliberate response from someone who has truly grasped His mercy. What is that mercy? Paul outlines it in Romans 1–11: All have sinned. All are guilty. But God, in Christ, justifies the ungodly. He gives peace, hope, freedom from sin, and adoption as sons. You are no longer condemned. Nothing can separate you from His love. That is mercy. So what is the proper response? Not partial devotion. Not Sunday-only religion. But *you*. Your body, your will, your whole life. That is not extreme; it is reasonable. Picture someone diving into the ocean to save you, only to drown in the process. Later, when asked how you responded, you say, "I said thank you." That would be unthinkable. The only reasonable response would be to live your life in honour of their sacrifice.

Now think of what Jesus did. He did not just risk His life; He gave it. He did not just save you from drowning; He saved you from hell. In light of that, giving yourself to God is not radical. It is the only sane response.

So yes, God is asking for your whole life. Not out of guilt but because it is the most thoughtful, grateful, and *reasonable* thing you could ever do.

Quote of the Day: Think of what Jesus did. He did not just risk His life; He gave it. He did not just save you from drowning; He saved you from hell. In light of that, giving yourself to God is not radical. It is the only sane response.

PERSONAL RESPONSE:

1. Do you view surrendering your whole life to God as a burden or as the logical response to His mercy?
2. In what specific ways are you offering your body, time, and will to God as a living sacrifice?
3. Have you been giving God partial devotion while holding parts of your life back from full surrender?

Daily Prayer: Lord, open my eyes to the depth of Your mercy and the weight of Your sacrifice for me. Help me respond, not with mere words or religious routines, but by offering my whole life to You. Let my surrender be thoughtful, joyful, and complete. Teach me to live each day as my reasonable service to You. In Jesus' name, amen.

Read the Bible in One Year: Psalms 40-42; Acts 27

THE HEART BEFORE THE HANDS

"And this they did, not as we hoped, but first gave their own selves to the Lord, and unto us by the will of God." 2 Corinthians 8:5

It is possible to give God something without giving Him yourself but impossible to give yourself and hold anything back. That is the difference between outward service and true surrender: one starts with your hands, the other with your heart.

Paul commended the Macedonians, not for the size of their offering, but for the sequence: *they first gave themselves to the Lord.* Before giving money, before supporting Paul, they surrendered their lives. That inward decision made their outward generosity powerful. You can serve in church, tithe faithfully, and still keep control of your life. You can volunteer while withholding your dreams, your desires, your time. God sees through it. He is not after performance; He is after possession. He wants you. Many confuse contribution with consecration. But God is not impressed with activity if He does not have ownership. When your heart is truly surrendered, your hands respond freely. Service flows from surrender. Paul adds, "and unto us by the will of God." Their submission to human leadership was an overflow of divine surrender. They were not serving Paul; they were serving Christ through Paul. If you wrestle with what God asks of you, the issue may not be the task; it may be the lack of surrender. When God has *you*, He can ask *anything*. Your answer will always be, "Yes, Lord." So let me ask you, my friend: Have you given yourself to the Lord? Not just your work or your worship, but *you*? Because until the heart is surrendered, the hands are limited. But when the heart comes first, service becomes joyful, willing, and powerful.

Quote of the Day: If you wrestle with what God asks of you, the issue may not be the task; it may be the lack of surrender. When God has *you*, He can ask *anything*. Your answer will always be, "Yes, Lord."

PERSONAL RESPONSE:

1. Have you truly given yourself to the Lord, or have you only been offering Him your service and resources?
2. What areas of your life are still under your control instead of fully surrendered to God?
3. Does your obedience to God flow from a surrendered heart or from pressure, routine, or expectation?

Daily Prayer: Dear Lord, I give You more than my time, my gifts, or my resources. I give You *me*. Take my heart, my will, and every part of my life. Let all my service flow from a place of deep surrender. Teach me to put my heart before my hands, and to serve You with joy and freedom, knowing that You already own me completely. In Jesus' name, amen.

Read the Bible in One Year: Psalms 43-45

THE DANGER OF ACTIVITY WITHOUT SURRENDER

"And Samuel said, Hath the LORD as great delight in burnt offerings and sacrifices, as in obeying the voice of the LORD? Behold, to obey is better than sacrifice, and to hearken than the fat of rams." 1 Samuel 15:22

It is one thing to be active in the things of God. It is another to be surrendered to God Himself. Activity can impress people. It can even deceive you. But without surrender, all your effort is empty. In God's Kingdom, service must flow from surrender, not the other way around.

You can serve God publicly and still not walk with Him privately. You can be known by men but unrecognized in heaven. That is what happens when you trade consecration for performance. Consider Saul. God told him to destroy the Amalekites completely, but Saul modified the instruction. He spared the king and kept the best animals. Then he built a monument to himself and claimed obedience. Saul's partial obedience was rebellion. He served without surrender, and it cost him the kingdom. Or look at Martha. Jesus was in her house, but she missed His presence in the name of serving Him. Mary, who sat at His feet, chose the "one thing needful" (Luke 10:42). Martha's hands were full, but her heart was dry. You can preach, plan, and pour yourself into ministry, yet still not be surrendered. You may carry gifts without depth, motion without transformation. God is not impressed by what you do until He owns who you are. Servanthood begins with surrender. You are not your own. You were bought with the blood of Jesus (1 Corinthians 6:19–20).

So here is the real question: **Have you given yourself to the Lord?** Not just your time, talents, or energy but you. Until He owns you, your service will be shallow. But once He does, your service will carry heaven's weight. Do not just give God your labour. **Give Him your life.**

Quote of the Day: God is not impressed by what you do until He owns who you are. Servanthood begins with surrender.

PERSONAL RESPONSE:

1. Have you been busy doing things for God while neglecting to truly surrender your heart and will to Him?
2. In what ways have you substituted outward service for inward obedience in your walk with God?
3. Are there areas in your life where you are still modifying God's instructions instead of obeying fully?

Daily Prayer: Dear Lord, I do not want to offer You empty activity or partial obedience. I give You not just my gifts or efforts; I give You myself. Break every form of pride, performance, or self-preservation in me. Let my service flow from true surrender, and let my life bring joy to Your heart. In Jesus' name, amen.

Read the Bible in One Year: Psalms 46-48; Acts 28

THE EVIDENCE OF A LIFE GIVEN TO GOD

"I am crucified with Christ: nevertheless I live; yet not I, but Christ liveth in me: and the life which I now live in the flesh I live by the faith of the Son of God, who loved me, and gave himself for me." Galatians 2:20

What does it look like to be a living sacrifice in real life? True surrender is not just a spiritual ideal; it shapes everything about you. It shows up in your speech, spending, service, and how you live when no one is watching.

At work, you serve with integrity, not just for promotion. You do not cut corners or work only when eyes are on you. You carry yourself as one working for the Lord, not for men.

In relationships, you love freely, forgive quickly, and submit to God's will. You stop manipulating and start ministering because your identity is anchored in Christ. In church, you are not seeking a spotlight; you are simply available. Whether you are sweeping the floor or preaching on a stage, it is the same to you. God owns you. You have stopped asking, "What's in it for me?" and now ask, "Lord, where do You need me?" In your finances, you tithe and give generously, not out of obligation but trust. You budget with eternity in mind. Money no longer defines your peace, God does. And in private, obedience becomes a lifestyle. You flee sin not from fear but from love. Even when tempted, you return to the altar. You have already surrendered, so obedience is not a negotiation, it is your default. Surrender is the end of spiritual debate. It silences the "must I?" and replaces it with "Yes, Lord." The decision has been made: *"I am the Lord's."* The bottom line is that surrender leaves a trail. You do not have to announce it. It shows, quietly, faithfully, consistently. That is the fruit God is after: not flawless performance, but a yielded heart.

Quote of the Day: Surrender is the end of spiritual debate. It silences the "must I?" and replaces it with "Yes, Lord." The decision has been made: *"I am the Lord's."*

PERSONAL RESPONSE:

1. Does your daily work reflect the values of someone who has fully surrendered to God, or are you still driven by personal ambition?
2. In your relationships, are you more focused on getting your way or submitting to God's will in how you love, forgive, and respond?
3. When no one is watching, do your private choices reflect a heart that has truly been placed on God's altar?

Daily Prayer: Dear Lord, I give myself to You again, completely and without reserve. Let my surrender show in every part of my life, even in secret. Take all of me, and let my lifestyle show that You own me. In Jesus' name, amen.

Read the Bible in One Year: Psalms 49-50; Romans 1

THE PRINCIPLE OF WHOLEHEARTED SERVICE

And it shall come to pass, if ye shall hearken diligently unto my commandments which I command you this day, to love the Lord your God, and to serve him with all your heart and with all your soul, that I will give you the rain of your land in his due season, the first rain and the latter rain, that thou mayest gather in thy corn, and thy wine, and thine oil." Deuteronomy 11:13-14

If there is one thing God does not accept, it is half-hearted service. He is not honoured by divided loyalty or lukewarm devotion. In *Deuteronomy 11:13*, He sets the standard of wholehearted service, and what follows? Rain in due season. A full harvest. Overflow. But the blessing only comes after the *wholehearted* service, not casual, convenient, or conditional service.

God is not impressed by busy activity if it comes from a divided soul. It is possible to serve publicly while holding back privately. That is why He says, "Serve Me with all your heart and all your soul."

To serve with all your heart means your emotions and affections are anchored in Him. He is not just your Redeemer; He is your Treasure. Your passion for Him is real, not mechanical.To serve with all your soul means your will is surrendered. You stop asking, "What do I want?" and start asking, "Lord, what would You have me do?"Half-hearted service is spiritual treason. You cannot serve God and still leave room for idols, self, or mammon (Matthew 6:24). God is not one of many priorities; He is your life.So let me ask you this question: Are you serving God because you love Him or because you want something from Him? Is your heart fully in, or still negotiating?When you give God your whole heart, He responds with His fullness. When you serve without reservation, He blesses without limitation. This is where the rain falls. This is where the blessing flows. This is the service that moves heaven.

Quote of the Day: When you give God your whole heart, He responds with His fullness. When you serve without reservation, He blesses without limitation.

PERSONAL RESPONSE:

1. Are you truly serving God with all your heart and all your soul, or are there areas of your life where your loyalty is still divided?
2. What hidden motivations might be holding you back from wholehearted service?
3. How would your decisions, relationships, and ministry involvement change if you fully surrendered your will to God?

Daily Prayer: Dear Lord, I give You all of me. Deliver me from lukewarm devotion. Let my life be marked by wholehearted love and service to You. In Jesus' name, I pray. Amen.

Read the Bible in One Year: Psalms 51-53; Romans 2

NOVEMBER 08

THE PROSPERITY OF OBEDIENT SERVANTS

"If they obey and serve him, they shall spend their days in prosperity, and their years in pleasures." Job 36:11

What a powerful promise we have in this verse, but note the condition: *if.* The promise is not automatic. It is reserved for those who obey and serve the Lord. This is not just about church attendance or spiritual activity. It is about living a life marked by consistent obedience and service. And the reward? Prosperity and pleasure, not as the world defines them, but as God does.

The Hebrew word translated "prosperity" is *tôb*, a rich word meaning goodness, well-being, wholeness in every area of life: materially, spiritually, emotionally, and relationally. It does not mean a life without trials, but a life defined by God's goodness, even in the midst of challenges.

Worried about marriage, money, purpose, or spiritual battles? The key is not anxiety; it is alignment. If you obey and serve the Lord, He takes responsibility for the rest. You will not miss what He has planned for you. You will not labour in vain. Your days will not be wasted.

The verse promises not *moments* of breakthrough, but *days* and *years*, meaning a sustained lifestyle of divine favour. The world may be in turmoil, but obedient servants live under God's covering.

So ask yourself: Am I obeying and serving God? Not in name only, but from a surrendered heart? If so, you do not need to chase blessings; they will chase you. You do not need to manipulate results; God will supply what you need.

Serve Him faithfully. Obey Him fully. And let His goodness define your days.

Quote of the Day: If you obey and serve the Lord, He takes responsibility for the rest.

PERSONAL RESPONSE:

1. Are there areas in your life where you have been serving God outwardly but neglecting to obey Him fully inwardly?
2. Do you view obedience and service as optional extras, or as the foundation for accessing God's promises?
3. What specific step of obedience is the Lord calling you to take today, and are you willing to respond promptly?

Daily Prayer: Dear Lord, I surrender every part of my life to You. Teach me to obey You fully and serve You faithfully, not for what I can get, but because You are worthy. Let my days be marked by Your goodness, and my years by Your pleasure, as I walk in total alignment with Your will. In Jesus' name, amen.

Read the Bible in One Year: Psalms 54-56; Romans 3

NOVEMBER 09

YOU ARE NOT DOING GOD A FAVOUR

"If these should hold their peace, the stones would immediately cry out." Luke 19:40

Let us settle it: you are not doing God a favour by serving Him. It is *mercy* that you even get to. God does not *need* your service but you desperately need *His blessing*. If you withhold your time, gifts, or devotion, God does not lose, but you do. If you won't serve Him, He can raise another. He is never stranded, but you are stranded without Him.

Many think that showing up or giving money in church is some great favour to God. But the privilege is not that He receives your service; it is that He *wants* it at all.

Look at King Saul in 1 Samuel 15. He disobeyed God's clear command and then tried to offer sacrifices to cover it up. God rejected him, not because he did nothing, but because he did it *his own way*. He lost everything because he thought partial obedience was enough.

Or the rich young ruler in Matthew 19. Jesus told him to sell all and follow but he walked away sorrowful. He did not just leave Jesus; he also left purpose, joy, and eternal reward.

Friend, if you won't praise God, stones will. If you won't serve Him, He will raise someone else. But you will be the one who missed it. You are not helping God by serving Him; you are helping *yourself*.

Quote of the Day: You are not doing God a favour by serving Him. It is *mercy* that you even get to.

PERSONAL RESPONSE:

1. Are you serving God with the awareness that it is a privilege, or have you begun to see your service as a favour you are doing for Him?
2. In what specific ways has pride, entitlement, or self-centeredness crept into your acts of service to God?
3. Have you ever walked away from a clear instruction from God because it seemed too costly? What did you lose in the process?

Daily Prayer: Dear Lord, thank You for the privilege of serving You. Forgive me for the times I served with pride or entitlement. Today, I surrender again: my gifts, my time, my heart. Use me as You will. Help me to serve with humility, gratitude, and full obedience. In Jesus' name, Amen.

Read the Bible in One Year: Psalms 57-59; Romans 4

NOVEMBER 10

NOT ALL BLESSINGS ARE GOD

"The blessing of the LORD, it maketh rich, and he addeth no sorrow with it."
Proverbs 10:22

Not everything that looks like a blessing is from God. Not every open door leads to peace. Some "blessings" are traps in disguise. The world offers prosperity, but it often comes with torment. The blessing of the Lord is different: it makes rich and adds no sorrow.

There is such a thing as counterfeit success: riches that rob you of rest, promotions that drain your soul, breakthroughs that come with breakdowns. People often envy others without knowing the price they paid: sleepless nights, spiritual harassment, inner emptiness. Many admire wealth without peace, success without surrender. But the real test of blessing is not how impressive it looks; it is the peace it brings. I have been invited to dedicate houses that were stunning but spiritually heavy. Beautiful mansions where no one sleeps well. Families tormented because they built without God. They chased success without obedience. And the result? Burden, not blessing. Hear this: if God did not give it, you will carry what He never intended for you. You may touch it, but it will not profit you. You may enjoy it briefly, but sorrow will come. That is why you must not envy the prosperity of the wicked or compromise your faith for flashy gain. Wait for the blessing of the Lord. Align with His will. Obey Him fully. Serve Him sincerely. Because when God blesses you, He brings peace, not pressure; rest, not regret; joy, not sorrow. What God gives, He guards. And what He blesses, He backs. That is the only kind of prosperity worth having.

Quote of the Day: The real test of blessing is not how impressive it looks; it is the peace it brings

PERSONAL RESPONSE:

1. Have you ever pursued or accepted an opportunity that looked like a blessing but later brought you sorrow or restlessness?
2. Are there any areas in your life right now where you are more focused on appearance and achievement than on obedience and alignment with God?
3. When you evaluate your definition of success, is it shaped more by God's peace or by the world's applause?

Daily Prayer: Heavenly Father, I ask for discernment to recognize the difference between true blessing and counterfeit success. Help me to never pursue what You have not ordained. Align my heart with Your will, and lead me into the kind of prosperity that brings peace, not sorrow. In Jesus' name, Amen.

Read the Bible in One Year: Psalms 60-62; Romans 5

SERVING GOD WITH SINCERITY AND TRUTH

"Now therefore fear the Lord, and serve him in sincerity and in truth: and put away the gods which your fathers served on the other side of the flood, and in Egypt; and serve ye the Lord." Joshua 24:14

This was not a casual remark. It was a parting charge from Joshua, a faithful leader who knew what true service looked like. He was not just asking Israel to serve God; he was commanding them to do it with *sincerity and truth.* And that remains God's standard today.

The Hebrew word for *sincerity* here means wholeness or integrity. It is the same word used in Leviticus for blemish-free sacrifices. God does not want half-effort, leftover devotion. He wants a heart that is *undivided*, a life that is fully His. You cannot serve God in sincerity while clinging to idols, pride, or self-will. Sincerity means God owns *every inch* of your life: your time, money, relationships, ambitions, and desires. Sincerity is not about how emotional you feel about God; it is about how honestly and completely your life belongs to Him, even when you feel nothing at all. *Truth*, on the other hand, speaks of firmness, faithfulness, and moral integrity. To serve God in truth is to remain *anchored*, consistent, and unshaken by trials, culture, or convenience. You do not retreat when it gets hard. You do not quit when it is unpopular. You do not switch loyalties when pressure comes. When Joshua said "put away the gods," he meant: no more divided service. No more secret idols. No more "God and..." loyalties. God is not seeking part-time followers. He wants *all* of you. Not just when it is easy, but even when it costs you everything.

So ask yourself honestly: **Is my service blemish-free and anchored? Or have I drawn lines that God cannot cross?** The Lord still calls for service in sincerity and truth. Nothing else will do.

Quote of the Day: God is not seeking part-time followers. He wants *all* of you.

PERSONAL RESPONSE:

1. Is your service to God truly free from blemish, or are there still areas of your life where your devotion is partial or compromised?
2. When challenges arise, does your commitment to God remain steady or does your faithfulness shift with circumstances?
3. Are there "gods of Egypt" or idols from your past that you still secretly cling to, even while claiming to serve the Lord?

Daily Prayer: Heavenly Father, I yield every part of my life to You. Cleanse my heart from divided loyalty and help me serve You in sincerity and in truth. Make my worship pure, my devotion steady, and my whole life a worthy offering. In Jesus' name, Amen.

Read the Bible in One Year: Psalms 63-65; Romans 6

NOVEMBER 12

BIBLICAL PORTRAITS OF WHOLEHEARTED SERVICE 1: ABRAHAM

"By faith Abraham, when he was called to go out into a place which he should after receive for an inheritance, obeyed; and he went out, not knowing whither he went." Hebrews 11:8

Sometimes, the call to serve God with your all can feel abstract or overwhelming until you see it lived out. That's why Scripture is full of real people, with real weaknesses, who made real sacrifices and walked in radical devotion to God. They were not superhumans. They were men and women like you, but they leaned on God's grace and gave Him their all.

For the next five days, we will look at five portraits of wholehearted service, one for each day. These are not fairy tales. These are real lives, real decisions, real devotion. And if they could do it, so can you, by the same grace of God. We begin today with the first example: Abraham.

If there is any man in Scripture who demonstrates what it means to trust God completely and serve Him with his all, it is Abraham. The Lord called him to leave everything familiar and follow a path he did not even know. And Abraham obeyed. No map, no guarantees, just a promise. Then, years later, when Isaac, the son of promise, finally arrived, God asked for him. *"Take now thy son… and offer him."* What kind of God asks for the very thing He gave? The God who is worthy of it all, the God who tests the heart to see if He still sits on the throne. Abraham passed the test, not because he was perfect, but because he was surrendered. That is the essence of service: you do not get to keep anything back. Abraham's obedience shows us that to serve God with your all, you must be ready to give Him your plans, your future, even your dearest relationships.

Quote of the Day: To serve God with your all, you must be ready to give Him your plans, your future, even your dearest relationships.

PERSONAL RESPONSE:

1. Are there areas of your life that you have found difficult to surrender to God?
2. Like Abraham, would you still obey if God asked you to give up something you deeply cherish, without explaining why?
3. What steps can you take this week to demonstrate practical, wholehearted obedience to God's call, even when the path is uncertain?

Daily Prayer: Heavenly Father, I surrender all to You. Like Abraham, help me to trust You completely and to obey without hesitation. Teach me to hold nothing back, for You are worthy of it all. In Jesus' name, Amen.

Read the Bible in One Year: Psalms 66-67; Romans 7

BIBLICAL PORTRAITS OF WHOLEHEARTED SERVICE 2: DAVID

"And when he had removed him, he raised up unto them David to be their king; to whom also he gave testimony, and said, I have found David the son of Jesse, a man after mine own heart, which shall fulfil all my will." Acts 13:22

David's life is a powerful testimony to the impact of passion, humility, and repentance in the service of God. He was not a perfect man; far from it. He committed grievous sins, including adultery and murder. Yet, what set David apart was not his moral record, but his heart posture. When he fell, he did not run from God; he ran to Him. When he sinned, he repented deeply, without excuses. When he succeeded, he gave all the glory to God. David was not flawless, but he was faithful in his affection for God.

This is what it means to be "a man after God's own heart." It means your heart always finds its way back to the throne. David served God through his music, through his leadership, through his courage in battle, and even through his repentance. He poured his soul into the Psalms, not just as a songwriter, but as a servant who longed for God's presence. Whether in the palace or the wilderness, David lived to honour God.

Wholehearted service is not about a spotless life. It is about a surrendered heart. If David, with all his flaws and failures, could serve God with his all, then what excuse do you have? God is still looking for hearts like David's. will He find one in you?

Quote of the Day: Wholehearted service is not about a spotless life. It is about a surrendered heart.

PERSONAL RESPONSE:

1. Like David, do you run to God in repentance when you fall, or do you retreat in shame and pride?

Is your service to God driven by deep love and longing for His presence, or merely by duty and appearances?

In what areas of your life can you begin to serve God more wholeheartedly like David did?

Daily Prayer: Dear Lord, give me a heart like David's: soft in repentance, bold in devotion, and wholly surrendered to You. Let my service to You flow from a deep, unwavering passion for Your presence. In Jesus' name, I pray. Amen.

Read the Bible in One Year: Psalms 68-69

BIBLICAL PORTRAITS OF WHOLEHEARTED SERVICE 3: PAUL

"But none of these things move me, neither count I my life dear unto myself, so that I might finish my course with joy, and the ministry, which I have received of the Lord Jesus, to testify the gospel of the grace of God." Acts 20:24

What kind of man says, *"I do not count my life dear unto myself"*? Only a man who has found something greater than life itself! The apostle Paul lived with a radical sense of purpose. After his encounter with Christ on the road to Damascus, everything changed. His priorities shifted. His ambitions died. His life was no longer his own. From that moment on, Paul's singular obsession was Christ and His gospel.

He endured brutal stonings, long imprisonments, shipwrecks, betrayals, hunger, beatings, and constant danger. Yet he referred to these sufferings as *"light afflictions"* because he saw them through the lens of eternity. Paul had already placed his life on the altar. He had settled it in his heart that comfort was not his goal; Christ was. Obedience was his measure of success, not popularity or ease.

This is the heart of true servanthood. To serve God with your all means you do not hold back, even when the cost is high. You embrace the cross. You accept suffering when it advances God's kingdom. You are willing to be spent for His glory.

Paul did not serve God on his own strength. It was the grace of God and the power of the Holy Spirit that enabled him. And friend, that same Spirit is available to you today. If Paul could serve like that, so can you, by that same grace.

Quote of the Day: To serve God with your all means you do not hold back, even when the cost is high.

PERSONAL RESPONSE:

2. What personal comforts or conveniences are you still clinging to that might be hindering your full obedience to Christ?
3. In what ways is your life currently reflecting an eternal perspective, like Paul's?
4. Are you willing to embrace hardship or sacrifice if it means advancing the kingdom of God?

Daily Prayer: Dear Lord, give me the same heart You gave Paul, a heart that counts nothing more precious than knowing and serving You. Help me to lay my life on the altar daily, to live for what matters most, and to serve You with unwavering devotion, no matter the cost. In Jesus' name, amen.

Read the Bible in One Year: Psalms 70-71; Romans 8

BIBLICAL PORTRAITS OF WHOLEHEARTED SERVICE 4: MARY

"And Mary said, Behold the handmaid of the Lord; be it unto me according to thy word. And the angel departed from her." Luke 1:38

Mary was a teenage girl with everything to lose: her reputation, her engagement, her future, even her life. In her culture, an unmarried pregnancy could bring shame, social rejection, or even death by stoning. Yet when the call of God came to her through the angel Gabriel, she said yes. Not because she had all the answers. Not because she knew how it would all work out. But because her heart was fully surrendered to the will of God.

"Be it unto me according to thy word." With those simple words, Mary stepped into the most demanding assignment ever given to a woman. She would carry the Son of God in her womb, endure public scrutiny, face the heartbreak of watching Him suffer, and yet remain faithful through it all. What gave her the strength? A heart that trusted God more than her own understanding.

Mary's life reminds us that wholehearted service is not always loud. It does not always involve a stage or spotlight. Sometimes, it looks like quiet obedience. Sometimes, it looks like humility that chooses surrender over control. When you say "yes" to God, even when it costs you, that is serving Him with your all. And God still honours that kind of surrender today.

Quote of the Day: When you say "yes" to God, even when it costs you, that is serving Him with your all. And God still honours that kind of surrender today.

PERSONAL RESPONSE:

1. Are there areas in your life where you are waiting to understand everything before you obey God?
2. What fears or uncertainties have been holding you back from fully surrendering to God's will?
3. Like Mary, are you willing to say "yes" to God even when His instructions do not align with your plans?

Daily Prayer: Dear Lord, I may not understand all that You are doing, but I trust You. Give me a heart like Mary's: humble, surrendered, and ready to say "yes" to Your will, no matter the cost. In Jesus' name, I pray. Amen.

Read the Bible in One Year: Psalms 72-73; Romans 9

BIBLICAL PORTRAITS OF WHOLEHEARTED SERVICE 5: JESUS

"Jesus saith unto them, My meat is to do the will of him that sent me, and to finish His work." John 4:34

Jesus is not just our Saviour; He is our Model Servant. He did not only come to die for us; He came to show us how to live in perfect obedience to the Father. Every step He took, every word He spoke, every miracle He performed was driven by one central passion: to do the will of God.

He said, "My meat is to do the will of Him that sent me, and to finish His work". That was not just a poetic statement; it was a defining reality. Jesus found His deepest satisfaction, not in comfort or applause, but in obedience. That is the heart of a true servant.

And even when that will demanded suffering, betrayal, and death on a cross, Jesus did not retreat. He prayed, "Not my will, but thine be done" (Luke 22:42). That is the ultimate expression of wholehearted service: surrender with no escape route. He obeyed the Father, even unto death, with no reservations, no conditions, and no negotiations.

If Jesus, the only begotten Son of God, could submit completely, how much more should we? To follow Him is to imitate Him. Wholehearted service is not an extra-credit option for super-Christians. It is the path that every true disciple must walk. Let Jesus' example lead you.

Quote of the Day: Wholehearted service is not an extra credit option for super - Christians. It is the path every true disciple must walk.

PERSONAL RESPONSE:

1. Are you truly satisfied by doing the will of God, or are you still chasing other sources of fulfilment?
2. In what areas of your life are you still struggling to say, "Not my will, but Yours be done"?
3. If wholehearted obedience to God cost you everything, would you still follow through like Jesus did?

Daily Prayer: Lord Jesus, You lived a life of perfect obedience and surrendered fully to the Father's will, even unto death. Teach me to follow in Your steps. Break every resistance in me, and make doing the will of God my deepest joy and highest goal. In your precious name, I pray. Amen.

Read the Bible in One Year: Psalms 74-76

YOU ARE NOT ALONE

"For our rejoicing is this, the testimony of our conscience, that in simplicity and godly sincerity, not with fleshly wisdom, but by the grace of God, we have had our conversation in the world, and more abundantly to you-ward." 2 Corinthians 1:12

Have you tried to serve God wholeheartedly and failed? Does offering everything to Him feel more like a burden than a blessing? If you answered yes to one or both of these questions, then hear this clearly: **you are not alone.**

Yes, God's standard is high, but He never expects you to meet it in your own strength. In our memory verse above, Paul said, *"...not with fleshly wisdom, but by the grace of God."* That means his wholehearted service was fuelled by grace, not grit.

In *Galatians 5:22–23*, "faithfulness" (which reflects sincere, consistent devotion) is listed as **fruit of the Spirit**. That means it is not self-produced; it is Spirit-grown. You do not serve God through willpower, but through surrender and dependence on the Holy Spirit.

The Holy Spirit is not a concept. He is your Helper. If you are born again, He lives in you, and He is working. You may not feel it, but He is making you more sincere, more faithful, more like Jesus.

1 Thessalonians 5:24 says, "Faithful is he that calleth you, who also will do it." Yes, the call is radical. But yes, **it is possible**. You can serve God with your all because He has already given you His.

So rise. Do not shrink back. The Spirit is with you, in you, and for you. And with Him, you can live a life that truly pleases God.

Quote of the Day: You do not serve God through willpower, but through surrender and dependence on the Holy Spirit.

PERSONAL RESPONSE:

1. In what areas of your life have you felt most discouraged about your ability to serve God wholeheartedly?
2. Are you trying to meet God's standard in your own strength, or are you relying daily on the help of the Holy Spirit?
3. How can you be more intentional this week in surrendering to the Spirit's work in your heart and actions?

Daily Prayer: Heavenly Father, thank You for calling me to serve You with my all. I confess that I cannot do it in my own strength. Fill me afresh with Your Holy Spirit and teach me to lean on Your grace. In Jesus' name, I pray. Amen.

Read the Bible in One Year: Psalms 77-78; Romans 10

A LESSON FROM THE SERVANTHOOD OF JESUS

"For even the Son of man came not to be ministered unto, but to minister, and to give his life a ransom for many." Mark 10:45

If anyone ever had the right to demand service from others, it was Jesus. He was the Son of God, God in the flesh, the Creator of the universe walking among His creation. He commanded storms, healed the sick, raised the dead, and multiplied bread for thousands. Legions of angels were at His disposal. Yet, with all that power, He made a startling choice: not to be served, but to serve.

Jesus did not use His authority for self-glory. Instead, He stooped to serve. He picked up a towel to wash dusty feet. He touched the untouchable, welcomed the outcast, wept with the grieving, bore the burdens of the broken, and ultimately laid down His life for people who did not even understand what He was doing. That is not weakness; it is power under control. That is true servanthood.

Unlike many today who turn influence into entitlement, Jesus chose meekness. "I am meek and lowly in heart," He said, not because He had no power, but because He had fully surrendered it to the Father's will. That is the difference between Christ-like ministry and carnal performance.

In the Kingdom of God, greatness is not measured by title or platform, but by towel and basin. Real servants are known by quiet sacrifice, hidden obedience, and costly love.

Quote of the Day: In the Kingdom of God, greatness is not measured by title or platform, but by towel and basin.

PERSONAL RESPONSE:

1. When was the last time you served someone quietly, without seeking recognition, applause, or reward?
2. How do you respond when service feels inconvenient or goes unnoticed? Does it reveal a servant's heart or a need for validation?
3. In what specific area of your life do you need to lay down entitlement and pick up the towel like Jesus?

Daily Prayer: Heavenly Father, I surrender my desire for recognition and control. Teach me to serve like Jesus, with meekness, humility, and love. Let my life reflect the posture of a true servant, even when no one is watching. In Jesus' name, I pray. Amen.

Read the Bible in One Year: Psalms 79-80; Romans 11

SERVANTHOOD AS THE BEGINNING OF TRUE LIFE

"And he sat down, and called the twelve, and saith unto them, If any man desire to be first, the same shall be last of all, and servant of all." Mark 9:35

You have not truly begun your journey until you have embraced the posture of a servant. Yes, you may have a title or recognition, but in the kingdom of God, life does not start until you bow low and choose to serve.

Servanthood is not the end; it is the beginning. It is the door that opens every other door. Until you assume this posture, your life remains surface-level, no matter your gifts or achievements.

Marriage thrives on service, not status. A husband who won't stoop to serve has missed the point. A wife who demands love but withholds it sabotages the very blessing she seeks. Mutual servanthood makes marriage flourish.

Parenting is no different. The moment a child is born, a servant is born. Influence comes from sacrificial example, not instructions. In ministry too, power flows through humility. People follow you when they see your scars, not your titles. Pride delays destinies. You cannot carry your crown and your cross at the same time. The cross comes first. If you are too big to serve, you are too small to lead.

Servanthood is not a punishment; it is the path to significance. It does not drain you; it fulfils you. And in losing yourself, you find your true life. Everything begins here. If you want to go far, start low. If you want to truly live, die to self. This is heaven's design. Embrace it.

Quote of the Day: If you are too big to serve, you are too small to lead.

PERSONAL RESPONSE

1. In what area of your life have you struggled to embrace the posture of a servant?
2. Are there titles, achievements, or personal ambitions that are standing in the way of you stooping low to serve others?
3. How willing are you to serve when no one is watching, when there is no applause, and when the task feels beneath you?

Daily Prayer: Lord, I lay down my pride, my titles, and my need to be seen. Teach me the way of the towel and basin. Break every resistance in me to humble service. Let my life begin anew from the ground of servanthood, and let me find true joy and fulfilment as I follow Christ in the lowly path. Amen. In Jesus' name, I pray. Amen.

Read the Bible in One Year: Psalms 81-83

HOW JESUS BECAME A SERVANT

"Who, being in the form of God, thought it not robbery to be equal with God: But made himself of no reputation, and took upon him the form of a servant, and was made in the likeness of men." Philippians 2:6–7

Pause and consider this: Jesus, equal with God, **made Himself of no reputation.** He did not cling to His divine status. He emptied Himself of privilege and applause, not out of compulsion, but by choice.

Imagine the Creator stepping into creation as a baby. The Commander of angels rejected by those He came to save. The One with all authority crucified like a criminal. And through it all, He took upon Himself **the form of a servant**.

Jesus did not just act like a servant; He became one. It was not a temporary gesture. It was an identity He embraced willingly. No one forced Him into it. He **took** it. And that is how true servanthood always begins: not by pressure, but by personal choice.

But here is the real issue: if there is one thing that keeps us from serving, it is pride. Ego resists it. Reputation fears it. We protect our image, even in ministry. Yet Jesus gave up all that we cling to, and invites us to do the same.

Servanthood is where pride dies and destiny begins. You are most like Christ when you choose to make yourself of no reputation. It is not about being seen or celebrated. It is about being faithful and obedient. So ask yourself: What am I still holding on to? What reputation do I need to release?

Jesus made Himself of no reputation. Will you?

Quote of the Day: Servanthood is where pride dies and destiny begins.

PERSONAL RESPONSE:

1. What reputation, title, or image are you still holding on to that makes it difficult for you to serve like Christ did?
2. In what areas of your life do you resist taking the lower place, even though you know God is calling you to humility?
3. Are there practical ways you can "take upon yourself the form of a servant" this week?

Daily Prayer: Lord Jesus, You made Yourself of no reputation and chose the form of a servant. Today, I lay down my pride, my need for recognition, and every title I hide behind. Teach me to walk in true humility. Help me to willingly take the lower place, not for show, but to reflect Your heart. Make me a servant like You. In your matchless name, I pray. Amen.

Read the Bible in One Year: Psalms 84-86; Romans 12

GREATNESS THROUGH SERVICE

"But it shall not be so among you: but whosoever will be great among you, let him be your minister." Matthew 20:26

If you want to understand how the Kingdom of God operates, begin with this truth: **the way up is down**. In the world, greatness is measured by status, applause, and possessions. But in God's Kingdom, greatness is defined by service.

In Matthew 20, the disciples argued about position, but Jesus turned their thinking upside down: *"Whoever wants to be great must be your servant."* Greatness, He taught, is not in being served, but in becoming the least.

Let's be honest. There is nothing wrong with wanting to be great. God wired you for significance. But how you pursue it is everything. If your ambition is about applause or recognition, you have missed the point. But if your longing for greatness drives you to your knees, to love deeper and serve wider, then you are seeing through Jesus' eyes.

Jesus lived true greatness. He knelt with a towel. He welcomed children. He touched lepers. He washed His disciples' feet. He died on a cross. **That is greatness.** And now He says, "Follow Me." The question is not *"Do you want to be great?"* It is *"Are you willing to serve?"* In God's Kingdom, you do not climb into greatness. You stoop into it.

So if you truly desire to carry God's glory, prepare your heart, not for a platform, but for a basin. Because here, **greatness is not seized. It is received. And only servants qualify.**

Quote of the Day: If you want to understand how the Kingdom of God operates, begin with this truth: **the way up is down**.

PERSONAL RESPONSE:

1. What does your current pursuit of greatness look like? Are you chasing recognition or embracing opportunities to serve?
2. In what specific ways can you stoop lower in your home, church, or workplace to reflect Christ's definition of greatness?
3. Are there hidden motives in your desire to be used by God that need to be surrendered to His way of humility and service?

Daily Prayer: Heavenly Father, I lay down my pride and worldly ambition. Teach me the way of true greatness. Make me a servant after Your heart. Let my life reflect Jesus, who came not to be served, but to serve. Amen.

Read the Bible in One Year: Psalms 87-88; Romans 13

CHRIST-CENTRED SERVANTS

"For we preach not ourselves, but Christ Jesus the Lord; and ourselves your servants for Jesus' sake." 2 Corinthians 4:5

This is the heartbeat of a true servant: *"We preach not ourselves."* Paul's words are not mere humility; they are a test. A test that reveals whether we serve Christ or subtly serve ourselves.

True servants do not draw attention to themselves. They do not preach to be seen or serve to be praised. Their message is Christ, not their opinions, style, or story. But today, ministry is increasingly being confused with personal branding. The pulpit has become a platform. The goal? Visibility, not obedience.

Self-promotion is not always loud. Sometimes, it wears a collar. Sometimes, it sings in the choir. But underneath, the motive is the same. *"Look at me."*

How do we "preach ourselves"? By chasing followers instead of faithfulness. By prioritizing image over anointing. By glorifying personal success in testimonies. By measuring impact through applause, not obedience. But the true servant of God deflects the spotlight. His joy is that people leave talking about Jesus, not about him.

"And whatsoever ye do, do it heartily, as to the Lord..." (Colossians 3:23). Whether preaching, leading, serving, or showing up, do it for Christ. He is your audience. He is your reward.

Why are you doing what you do? Is it for Jesus or is it about you? God sees beyond performance. He sees the heart. And in the end, only one Name will matter, and it is not yours.

Purge your heart of self. Serve for Christ's sake. Point to Him in everything. Because only what is done for Jesus will last.

Quote of the Day: Why are you doing what you do? Is it for Jesus or is it about you?

PERSONAL RESPONSE:

1. When people interact with your ministry, leadership, or service, who gets the spotlight, Jesus or you?
2. Are there areas in your life where you are subtly promoting yourself under the banner of "serving God"?
3. What changes can you make this week to shift the focus of your service more fully onto Christ?

Daily Prayer: Heavenly Father, purify my heart from every trace of self-exaltation. Strip me of the desire to be seen, praised, or promoted. Let Christ be my message, my motive, and my reward. Help me serve to others with humility and sincerity, for Jesus' sake alone. Amen.

Read the Bible in One Year: Psalms 89-90; Romans 14

THE ANOINTING MAKES THE DIFFERENCE

"And it shall come to pass in that day, that his burden shall be taken away from off thy shoulder, and his yoke from off thy neck, and the yoke shall be destroyed because of the anointing." Isaiah 10:27

What truly makes the difference in your walk with God is the anointing. Settle this in your heart: you cannot fulfil your calling, break yokes, or sustain victory without it. The anointing is not a luxury; it is a necessity. It is what separates powerless religion from supernatural life. The yoke shall be destroyed because of the anointing, not because of money, connections, motivation, or even hard work. The anointing is what destroys yokes, lifts burdens, and causes real breakthrough. This is why you must not chase only open doors, opportunities, or platforms. All those things may come, but without the anointing, nothing in your life will carry eternal weight. You may be successful outwardly and still see things fall apart. Without the anointing, you can have a beautiful family, a thriving business, or a growing ministry and still feel empty and fruitless. The anointing is the game-changer. It brings heaven's power into human affairs. Yet many are serving zealously, but powerlessly, because they are not anointed. And so they burn out. They do the right things but get wrong results. Talent is not enough. Passion is not enough. If you are not anointed, you will hit ceilings you cannot break and face yokes you cannot lift. We live in a world full of invisible battles, and only the anointing wins them. Without it, your voice is noise. But with it, your whisper carries power. Your life becomes a channel for deliverance.

Do not try to live or serve without the anointing. Seek it. Treasure it. Depend on it. It makes all the difference.

Quote of the Day: The anointing is not a luxury; it is a necessity. It is what separates powerless religion from supernatural life.

PERSONAL RESPONSE:

1. In what areas of your life have you been relying on talent, effort, or connections instead of the anointing?
2. How can you practically posture your heart to seek and depend on the Holy Spirit's power daily?
3. What signs in your service or spiritual life suggest that you may be operating without fresh oil from God?

Daily Prayer: Dear Lord, I confess that I cannot fulfil my calling without Your anointing. I surrender my strength, ambition, and strategies. Fill me afresh with Your Spirit. Let Your power rest on me and destroy every yoke in and around my life. Make me a vessel that carries heaven's presence everywhere I go. In Jesus' name, Amen.

Read the Bible in One Year: Psalms 91-93; Romans 15

NOVEMBER 24

WHAT IS THE ANOINTING?

"Then Samuel took the horn of oil, and anointed him in the midst of his brethren: and the Spirit of the Lord came upon David from that day forward. So Samuel rose up, and went to Ramah." 1 Samuel 16:13

The anointing is the power of God flowing through a person. It is heaven's ability working in human vessels, not a feeling, a goosebump, or a sensation, but visible, supernatural enablement from God.

In Scripture, those anointed were set apart and empowered. When David was anointed in our memory verse, *"the Spirit of the Lord came mightily upon him from that day forward."* That is what the anointing does. It marks and empowers. Think of Samson tearing lions apart (Judges 14:6), Elijah calling down fire (1 Kings 18:36–38), or Peter preaching one sermon that saved 3,000 souls (Acts 2:41). The difference was the anointing. The anointing is what makes your words carry weight, your labour yield results, and your life transmit God's power. It does not merely enhance natural gifts; it transcends them. It turns fishermen into apostles, shepherd boys into kings, and ordinary people into vessels of divine glory. And here is the truth: when you are anointed, you cannot live ordinarily. You carry a divine distinction. The anointing causes you to rise where others fall, to stand where others faint. In a world filled with invisible chains, strange battles, and demonic pressure, God is not seeking polished professionals. He is seeking anointed servants. The anointing is not inherited. It is received through divine encounter and cultivated through surrender, obedience, and humility. It is God's unmistakable mark upon a life, and it breaks yokes, lifts burdens, and ushers victory. This anointing is not for the proud or the platform-seekers. It is for those who choose the servant's path. So ask yourself today: Do I hunger for the anointing? Because without it, you will struggle. But with it, nothing is impossible. **Quote of the Day:** The anointing is what makes your words carry weight, your labour yield results, and your life transmit God's power.

PERSONAL RESPONSE:

1. Are you relying on your natural abilities, or are you consciously depending on the anointing of the Holy Spirit in your daily life and service?
2. In what areas of your life are you currently operating without the anointing, and what difference might it make if you surrendered those areas to God?
3. Have you embraced the posture of humility and servanthood that attracts the anointing, or are pride and self-reliance keeping you from receiving God's power?

Daily Prayer: Dear Lord, I humble myself before You and ask for a fresh outpouring of Your anointing. Strip me of self-reliance, and empower me to serve with Your strength, walk in Your authority, and carry Your presence everywhere I go. In Jesus' name, amen.

Read the Bible in One Year: Psalms 94-96

A LESSON FROM ELISHA

"But Jehoshaphat said, Is there not here a prophet of the Lord, that we may enquire of the Lord by him? And one of the king of Israel's servants answered and said, Here is Elisha the son of Shaphat, which poured water on the hands of Elijah." 2 Kings 3:11

Elisha's story offers a powerful reminder that in God's Kingdom, the anointing flows not to the most visible, but to the most submitted. When the kings of Israel, Judah, and Edom needed a prophet, Elisha was recommended, not because of fame or title, but because he *"poured water on the hands of Elijah"*.

That simple act of service became his qualification for spiritual authority. He did not begin with a platform; he began with a towel. He was not pursuing recognition; he was ministering quietly to a man of God, even when that man was unpopular and persecuted. Elisha's story tells us: *You do not need a title to carry power. You do not have to be seen to be anointed.*

In a culture obsessed with status and visibility, Elisha reminds us that God values faithfulness in obscurity. Before Elisha ever performed miracles, he served. Before the mantle fell, he poured water. Before he received his own platform, he was faithful with another man's vision.

This is the principle Jesus echoed in Luke 16:12: *"If ye have not been faithful in that which is another man's, who shall give you that which is your own?"* God's power follows a servant's posture.

Elisha's life confronts us with a question: Are you willing to serve when no one is watching? Are you content to be known in heaven, even if the crowd never applauds you? Because in the Kingdom, *mantles fall on servants*. Heaven recognizes towels more than titles. And the one who pours water today may be the one who carries power tomorrow.

Quote of the Day: God's power follows a servant's posture.

PERSONAL RESPONSE:

1. Are you willing to serve faithfully behind the scenes, even when no one notices or applauds you?
2. Have you been more focused on seeking recognition than on cultivating a servant's heart?
3. What "Elijah" has God placed in your life for you to serve, and how faithfully are you serving them?

Daily Prayer: Lord, teach me to serve with humility like Elisha. Strip me of every desire for applause, and give me the heart that delights in quiet faithfulness. May I be found worthy to carry Your anointing, not for status, but for Your glory. In Jesus' name, I pray. Amen.

Read the Bible in One Year: Psalms 97-99; Romans 16

NOVEMBER 26

HOW SERVANTHOOD QUALIFIES YOU FOR THE OIL

"I have found David my servant; with my holy oil have I anointed him." Psalm 89:20

God did not say, "I have found David the king," or "the psalmist." He said, *"my servant."* That is what moved God's heart. Servanthood was David's qualification for the anointing. Not charisma. Not title. Not popularity. Just a servant heart.

Today, many seek the anointing without embracing the servant's posture. But God anoints function, not status. He is not impressed by pedigree or platforms. He is looking for those who pour water on others' hands. That is what made Elisha's name known in heaven (2 Kings 3:11). David did not begin in a palace but in a pasture. Overlooked by men, yet chosen by God. When Jesse sent him on an errand to deliver food (1 Samuel 17:17), David obeyed and walked straight into destiny. Goliath was not defeated by a spotlight-seeker but by a servant. The anointing is not a badge of honour; it is heaven's empowerment for those who are willing to carry others' burdens. Many want to lead but have never served. They want the oil without the towel. But God resists the proud and exalts the humble. Always. Even in 1 Chronicles 17:7–8, God reminded David: *"I took you from following sheep…"* He did not ignore David's small beginnings. He celebrated them. Why? Because *service invites elevation.* God is still searching today: *"I have found…"* Who will He find? Not celebrities but servants. Those who bend low, who lead quietly, who serve faithfully. If you desire divine power, take up the towel. Lay down your title. Serve like David. And heaven will respond with holy oil.

Quote of the Day: The anointing is not a badge of honour; it is heaven's empowerment for those who are willing to carry others' burdens.

PERSONAL RESPONSE:

1. Are you more eager to be seen as a leader or more willing to be found faithful as a servant?
2. What small, unnoticed tasks are currently before you, and are you embracing them as divine opportunities?
3. Have you been chasing the anointing without embracing the servanthood?

Daily Prayer: Dear Lord, make me the kind of servant You can anoint. Strip me of every selfish ambition, every prideful desire, and teach me to embrace humble service with joy and faithfulness. Let my heart be found faithful in the sheepfold, and may my life attract Your holy oil, not for my fame but for Your glory. In Jesus' name, Amen.

Read the Bible in One Year: Psalms 100-102; 1 Corinthians 1

DIMENSIONS OF THE SERVANT'S ANOINTING 1: STRENGTH FOR ASSIGNMENT

"I have found David my servant; with my holy oil have I anointed him. With whom My hand shall be established; also My arm shall strengthen him." Psalm 89:20-21

In Psalm 89:20, the Bible speaks of God anointing David with holy oil. In verses 21–36, we see what that anointing accomplished in his life. If you look closely at these verses, you'll find at least four key dimensions of the servant's anointing. That will be our focus for the next four days, one dimension for each day. Today, we begin with the first: **strength for assignment.** The first effect of the anointing in David's life was divine strength. God Himself declared, *"My arm shall strengthen him."* This is not physical stamina; it is supernatural enablement. The anointing gives you divine strength to carry out divine assignments. Without it, even simple tasks become exhausting. You may be talented and skilled, but without the anointing, you will still be overwhelmed. David faced lions, bears, giants, and endless battles, not because he was the strongest, but because the anointing made him strong.

This strength was not given to him for entertainment; it was entrusted to him because God had found a servant. Servants are the only ones God can trust with power. Why? Because they do not use it for themselves. You cannot pour strength into someone who won't use it to serve God's will. That is why God said, *"I have found David My servant"*, not David the warrior or David the worshipper, *"and with My holy oil have I anointed him."* When God finds a servant, He supplies strength.

Quote of the Day: The anointing gives you divine strength to carry out divine assignments. Without it, even simple tasks become exhausting.

PERSONAL RESPONSE:

1. In what specific area of your life or calling do you feel overwhelmed right now, and could it be that you are trying to carry the load without the anointing?
2. Are you positioning yourself as a servant whom God can trust with divine strength, or are you still pursuing your own agenda?
3. How have you been using your God-given abilities. Are they tools for service or platforms for self-promotion?

Daily Prayer: Dear Lord, make me the kind of servant You can trust. Strengthen me with Your arm and anoint me with Your holy oil, that I may carry out every assignment You have given me with divine enablement. In Jesus' name, Amen.

Read the Bible in One Year: Psalms 103-104; 1 Corinthians 2

DIMENSIONS OF THE SERVANT'S ANOINTING 2: VICTORY OVER ENEMIES

"I have found David my servant; with my holy oil have I anointed him. The enemy shall not outwit him, nor the son of wickedness afflict him. I will beat down his foes before his face, and plague those who hate him." Psalm 89:20, 22–23

There is a level of victory that cannot be explained by skill, strategy, or human connection. It is a kind of victory that defies logic, breaks limitations, and silences enemies, not because the person is the most qualified, but because they are anointed. David is a classic example. Scripture never records that he lost a single battle. This was not because he was the most trained warrior or had the largest army. It was because God had anointed him. The anointing placed a divine shield over his life. God declared, "I will plague those who hate him," and He backed that promise with action. David's victory was not rooted in technique; it was anchored in divine favour.

We live in a world filled with yokes, invisible chains, generational curses, and spiritual battles. You can be wealthy and still be bound. You can be brilliant and still be tormented. The only force that guarantees real and lasting freedom is the anointing. It destroys yokes. It breaks chains. It secures victory.

But here is the key: David's anointing flowed from his heart of service. Before he ever wielded a sword, he played the harp in Saul's court. Before he commanded armies, he carried bread to his brothers. Servanthood always precedes divine victory.

Quote of the Day: The only force that guarantees real and lasting freedom is the anointing. It destroys yokes. It breaks chains. It secures victory.

PERSONAL RESPONSE:

1. In what areas of your life are you relying on human strategy or effort instead of the anointing of God?
2. Have you embraced a posture of servanthood that qualifies you for divine victory, or are you waiting to be promoted before you begin to serve?
3. What signs in your life today suggest that your victories are being powered by God's anointing and not your own strength?

Daily Prayer: Heavenly Father, I surrender every battle of my life to You. Anoint me afresh and give me victory that no man can explain. Let Your power break every yoke, frustrate every enemy, and preserve me through every season, not because I am strong, but because I am Yours. In Jesus' name, amen.

Read the Bible in One Year: Psalms 105-106; 1 Corinthians 3

DIMENSIONS OF THE SERVANT'S ANOINTING 3: DIVINE FAVOUR AND PRESERVATION

"I have found David my servant; with my holy oil have I anointed him. My faithfulness and My mercy shall be with him, and in My name his horn shall be exalted." Psalm 89:20, 24

The anointing brought David divine favour. God declared, "My mercy shall be with him". This was not ordinary favour; it was covenant mercy, a divine commitment to show kindness even when David failed. The anointing placed David under an open heaven where God's loyalty to him surpassed human understanding. Mercy followed him, not because he was perfect, but because he was positioned as a servant. That is the mystery of favour: it is not earned through performance, but accessed through posture.

When the anointing rests upon a servant, God's name becomes their shield and banner. He said, "In My name shall his horn be exalted." That is promotion without striving. Honour without manipulation. Elevation without campaigning. David rose to kingship not by lobbying, but by loving. Not by fighting for position, but by being faithful in obscurity. That is how the anointing works. It lifts the lowly, exalts the humble, and decorates the hidden. Many today chase favour by chasing men, networking endlessly, and exhausting themselves trying to be seen. But God's favour is not earned that way. It comes to those who serve faithfully when no one is watching. When you pour yourself out in secret, God marks you in heaven and rewards you openly. The pathway to true favour is still the same: humility, faithfulness, and the servant's heart.

Quote of the Day: When the anointing rests upon a servant, God's name becomes their shield and banner.

PERSONAL RESPONSE:

1. Are you actively serving others in humility, or are you waiting to be recognized before you engage fully?
2. In what areas of your life do you seek favour and promotion? Are you trusting God's process or trying to make things happen by your own effort?
3. When corrected or overlooked, do you respond like a servant with a yielded heart, or like someone entitled to a platform?

Daily Prayer: Heavenly Father, I surrender my desire for recognition and promotion. Let Your anointing rest upon me as I serve in humility. Exalt me in Your name and surround my life with Your covenant mercy. In Jesus' name, Amen.

Read the Bible in One Year: Psalms 107-109; 1 Corinthians 4

NOVEMBER 30

DIMENSIONS OF THE SERVANT'S ANOINTING 4: ENDURING LEGACY

"I have found David my servant; with my holy oil have I anointed him. I will set his hand over the sea, and his right hand over the rivers... My covenant I will not break, nor alter the word that has gone out of My lips... His seed also I will make to endure forever..." Psalm 89:20, 25, 34, 36

The final dimension of the servant's anointing that I would like to draw your attention to is **legacy**. The anointing does not just empower you for the moment; it secures your future, establishes your impact, and preserves your relevance long after you are gone. It is possible to be powerful today and forgotten tomorrow. But when the anointing rests on a true servant, their influence outlives them.

Think of Elisha. Even after his death, his bones still carried the power of God (2 Kings 13:21). A dead man came back to life simply by touching Elisha's bones. That is legacy. That is not ordinary gifting or charisma. That is the residue of a life spent in selfless service to God.

In 1 Chronicles 17:7–8, God reminded David, *"I took you from the pasture, from following the sheep, and made you ruler over my people Israel."* David did not climb the throne by ambition; he was lifted by the anointing, which had found him faithful in service. His legacy was not built on titles or accomplishments; it was rooted in his servant heart.

You must understand: **servanthood is the soil in which legacy grows.** If nothing lasting is growing through you, perhaps nothing has died in you. Everyone wants impact, but few want to serve. Yet only servants receive the kind of anointing that echoes in eternity.

Quote of the Day: When the anointing rests on a true servant, their influence outlives them.

PERSONAL RESPONSE:

1. Are you more focused on building a platform for yourself or leaving behind a legacy of faithful service to God?
2. Have you embraced the kind of selfless, behind-the-scenes service that God uses to shape a lasting legacy?
3. What steps can you begin taking today to serve others in a way that reflects Christ and builds something that will outlive you?

Daily Prayer: Father, I lay down every desire for fleeting recognition and ask You to anoint me for lasting impact. Let my life become a seed of faithful service that bears fruit beyond my time. Help me to serve in such a way that generations after me will be touched by the residue of Your presence upon my life. In Jesus' name, amen.

Read the Bible in One Year: Psalms 110-112; 1 Corinthians 5

DECEMBER

WELCOME TO THE MONTH OF SUPERNATURAL LIVING

PROPHETIC DECREE

I decree that this month you are being redefined for Kingdom greatness through the spirit of servanthood. Every trace of pride, self-promotion, and worldly ambition is replaced with the humility and strength of Christ, the Servant King. You will walk the narrow road of true greatness, measured not by titles or applause, but by how deeply you serve and follow Jesus. The Holy Spirit will awaken in you a passion to live, lead, and labour like Christ. You will carry the anointing that rests on the lowly, with favour following you as you choose the towel over the throne. Each day will bring revelation, transformation, and a renewed longing to serve, as God entrusts you with divine assignments and eternal impact.

SUPERNATURAL LIVING

What does it truly mean to live supernaturally in a natural world? Why is there such a hunger in today's world for what lies beyond the physical? The cry for the supernatural echoes across generations, cultures, and nations, evident in the surge of mysticism, occultism, and alternative spiritualities. Deep within every human heart is a longing to touch something greater, something divine. That longing was placed there by God.

As a child of God, you were not designed to live by natural limitations. The moment you received Christ, you were born into a higher realm. You received the divine nature of God. That nature qualifies you not just to *believe* in the supernatural but to *live* it. Supernatural living is not reserved for a few elite Christians; it is the inheritance and responsibility of every believer. It is how we reflect heaven's realities here on Earth and fulfil God's mandate upon our lives.

This 31-day devotional is your invitation into that reality. Each day offers you fresh insight, prophetic encouragement, practical instructions, and powerful scriptural truths to help you live above the ordinary. You will also find daily prayers to stir your spirit and personal reflection questions to align your life with heaven's purpose.

Whether you are new to the faith or a seasoned believer, this devotional will awaken in you a new hunger for God's power, presence, and possibilities. As you journey through these pages, expect transformation, expect miracles, and expect to walk in the supernatural.

Welcome to *Supernatural Living*. Your journey beyond limits begins now!

TABLE OF CONTENTS

WALKING IN THE SUPERNATURAL Part 1

"Jesus answered and said to him, "Most assuredly, I say to you, unless one is born again, he cannot see the kingdom of God." John 3:3

In my experience, I have found that many people deeply desire to walk in the supernatural. This longing often drives them to seek supernatural experiences outside of God. But Jesus, in John 3:3, told Nicodemus that no one can access the supernatural without being born again. Redemption through the blood of Jesus is the gateway into this divine realm. Through Christ, we gain access to God, in whom all things consist.

However, salvation is only the beginning. To truly walk in the supernatural, you must journey beyond conversion and begin a consistent walk with God. The Bible says Enoch walked with God until he was taken up into heaven (Genesis 5:24). Likewise, Elijah's supernatural life was so intense that God took him away in a chariot of fire.

The Apostles, after encountering the risen Christ, operated in the supernatural and turned the world upside down. Jesus Himself walked on water, multiplied food, and suspended natural laws. He even promised in John 14:12 that those who believe in Him would do greater works. That promise still stands today.

God is the source of the supernatural. Your role is to engage it through two things: faith and a conscious walk with God. Hebrews 11, the Hall of Faith, shows that every supernatural act was performed "by faith." You too can walk in the supernatural if you believe God's Word and act on it. The same power that worked in Jesus and the Apostles is available to you today.

Quote of the Day: To truly walk in the supernatural, you must journey beyond conversion and begin a consistent walk with God.

PERSONAL RESPONSE:

1. Have you truly experienced the new birth that grants access to the supernatural life in Christ?
2. In what areas of your life do you need to begin walking by faith rather than by sight?
3. What specific steps can you take today to deepen your daily walk with God and align with His supernatural purposes?

Daily Prayer: Heavenly Father, I believe You are the God of the supernatural. Help me to walk by faith, live in obedience, and experience the fullness of Your power at work in and through me. In Jesus' name, amen.

Read the Bible in One Year: Psalms 116-118; 1 Corinthians 7

WALKING IN THE SUPERNATURAL Part 2

"And they went out and preached everywhere, the Lord working with them and confirming the word through the accompanying signs. Amen." Mark 16:20

In yesterday's devotional, we established the fact that walking in the supernatural begins with being born again and walking by faith. However, new birth is just the entry point. To operate effectively and consistently in the supernatural, you must now grow in spiritual maturity and deepen your journey with God.

The Word of God is your first training ground. As you stay rooted in the Scriptures, you begin to see your true identity and authority in Christ. You cannot walk in what you have not seen in God's Word. Abraham's ability to walk into God's promise began when he lifted his eyes and saw what God was offering (Genesis 13:14–15). Likewise, you must see what has been freely given to you in Christ. The second vital key is the Holy Spirit. He is the Custodian of the supernatural. Jesus did not perform a single miracle until He returned in the power of the Spirit (Luke 4:14). In the same way, you must be filled with the Holy Spirit, stay in fellowship with Him, and yield daily to His leading. Thirdly, supernatural exploits demand a Spirit-filled life grounded in the Word. Genesis 1 shows that creation was a fusion of the Word and the Spirit. So also must your life be a living expression of Spirit and truth. If you are born again, then the supernatural is your inheritance. But to walk in it daily, you must grow in the Word, yield to the Spirit, and deepen your walk with God. Do not just admire the supernatural, walk in it until it becomes your new normal.

Quote of the Day: If you are born again, then the supernatural is your inheritance. But to walk in it daily, you must grow in the Word, yield to the Spirit, and deepen your walk with God.

PERSONAL RESPONSE:

1. Are you actively feeding on God's Word to understand your authority and inheritance in Christ?
2. In what ways are you cultivating a deeper relationship with the Holy Spirit as the key to supernatural living?
3. How intentional are you about growing in spiritual maturity so you can handle deeper dimensions of the supernatural?

Daily Prayer: Heavenly Father, thank You for the gift of salvation and the privilege of walking in the supernatural. I ask for grace to grow in the knowledge of Your Word and to walk daily in deep fellowship with the Holy Spirit. Teach me to yield fully to You so that the supernatural becomes my normal experience. In Jesus' name, amen.

Read the Bible in One Year: Psalms 119

DECEMBER 03

SUPERNATURAL HELP

"But when the Helper comes, whom I will send to you from the Father, the Spirit of truth, who proceeds from the Father, he will bear witness about." John 15:26

Do you know why many faithful believers still end up living a defeated life? It is because they fail to embrace the supernatural help of the Holy Spirit.

The Holy Spirit is the believer's advantage for living an overcoming and victorious life. When you do not allow Him to help you, you short-change yourself of divine provisions and heavenly resources. He is your help in moments of weakness, struggle, and anxiety. It is through the supernatural help of the Holy Spirit that you experience the richness of God's grace.

In times of trouble, you must recognize the role of the Holy Spirit as your ever-present help. He is all you need to overcome the obstacles before you. Without the Holy Spirit, you cannot access the supply of grace because He is the Spirit of grace.

Friend, divine help for the believer comes only through the Holy Spirit. It is futile to trust in the arm of flesh. People may disappoint you, but the Holy Spirit never will.

Are you burdened with pain, anxiety, or helplessness? It is time to return to your Helper and stop looking for man-made solutions. The Holy Spirit is your surest help. Learn to lean on Him constantly, especially in times of crisis.

Quote of the Day: The Holy Spirit is the believer's advantage for living an overcoming and victorious life.

PERSONAL RESPONSE:

1. In what areas of your life have you been trying to succeed without relying on the Holy Spirit's help?
2. How often do you consciously invite the Holy Spirit into your daily struggles, decisions, and weaknesses?
3. What practical steps can you take to deepen your dependence on the Holy Spirit rather than on human strength?

Daily Prayer: Holy Spirit, I acknowledge that I need You. Help me to stop leaning on my own strength and to trust fully in Your supernatural help. Teach me to walk in constant dependence on You, especially in moments of weakness and uncertainty. In Jesus' name, amen.

Read the Bible in One Year: Psalms 120; 1 Corinthians 8

SUPERNATURAL POWER

"But you shall receive power when the Holy Spirit has come upon you, and you shall be witnesses to Me in Jerusalem, and all Judea and Samaria, and to the end of the Earth." Acts.1:8

Have you ever wondered why Jesus gave a strict instruction to His disciples to *wait* in Jerusalem until they had received power from on high (Luke 24:49)? It was not a suggestion; it was a command. Why? Because to live out the supernatural life God has called you to, you need the supernatural power of God. Without it, your Christian walk will lack fire, your witness will lack impact, and your assignment will lack the force of Heaven behind it.

The power of God is not a luxury; it is a necessity. It is what enables you to fulfil divine purpose and remain relevant in your generation. Without it, you become vulnerable to the forces of darkness that govern the natural world. But through the power of God, you can live above limitation and walk in dominion.

So how do you access this power? It comes through the anointing of the Holy Spirit. When you receive the Holy Spirit, you receive access to the supernatural power of God. But receiving the Spirit is not a one-time event; it is a daily relationship, and it is sustained by prayer. A prayerless believer will remain powerless.

If you truly desire to walk in power, become a person of deep prayer. Cry out today for the baptism of the Holy Spirit. That is your gateway into the fullness of God's supernatural power.

Quote of the Day: The power of God is not a luxury; it is a necessity. It is what enables you to fulfil divine purpose and remain relevant in your generation.

PERSONAL RESPONSE:

1. Have you received the baptism of the Holy Spirit, or are you trying to fulfill your divine assignment without God's power?
2. In what ways is your current prayer life preparing you to walk in supernatural power?
3. What distractions or habits might be hindering you from experiencing the fullness of the Holy Spirit's anointing?

Daily Prayer: Lord Jesus, I recognize that I cannot fulfil Your purpose for my life without Your power. Baptize me afresh with the Holy Spirit and fire. Stir in me a deep hunger for prayer and intimacy with You, that I may walk in the supernatural and live a life that glorifies You. In your mighty name, I pray. Amen.

Read the Bible in One Year: Psalms 121-122; 1 Corinthians 9

MAKING THE SUPERNATURAL YOUR NATURAL LIFE

"Abide in me, and I in you. As the branch cannot bear fruit of itself unless it abides in the vine, so neither can you unless you abide in me." John 15:4

Are you tired of living an ordinary life? Tired of rising and falling? Do you long to make a supernatural impact on your generation? There is a solution to your struggle.

Many people believe it is impossible to live a supernatural life in this natural world. But that mindset is a lie from the enemy, designed to keep you from stepping into your God-given potential.

There are severe limitations in living a merely natural life. Without the supernatural power of God backing you, you cannot make a lasting spiritual impact. No natural man can overcome the devil in his own strength. That is why Satan resists any believer seeking to live a supernatural life.

As a child of God, a vital key to living supernaturally is abiding in Christ. You must constantly pray for the grace to remain in Him because steadfastness is only possible through communion with God. Prayer is essential. Without it, you will struggle to live above sin and opposition.

In addition to prayer, you must cultivate unwavering faith. Believe that it is indeed possible to live a supernatural life, no matter what others think. With God, all things are possible, including making the supernatural your everyday reality.

Quote of the Day: No natural man can overcome the devil in his own strength. That is why Satan resists any believer seeking to live a supernatural life.

PERSONAL RESPONSE:

1. Are you actively abiding in Christ, or are you trying to bear fruit while disconnected from the Source?
2. What changes can you make in your daily routine to cultivate a deeper life of prayer and dependence on the Holy Spirit?
3. Do you truly believe that living a supernatural life is possible for you, or have you accepted a limited, natural existence?

Daily Prayer: Lord Jesus, I choose to abide in You. Help me to remain steadfast in prayer and faith, and teach me to walk in the supernatural as my daily reality. Let Your power work in me and through me, so that my life brings glory to You. In your precious name, I pray. Amen.

Read the Bible in One Year: Psalms 123-125; 1 Corinthians 10

DECEMBER 06

SUPERNATURAL IDENTITY

"Then God said, 'Let Us make man in Our image, according to Our likeness; let them have dominion over the fish of the sea, over the birds of the air, and over the cattle, over all the earth and over every creeping thing that creeps on the earth.'" Genesis 1:26

What is your identity? Your identity defines who you are, why you exist, and what sets you apart. According to Scripture, your true identity originates from God. In Genesis 1:26, God declares that you were created in His image and likeness, meaning you are a reflection of Him on Earth. You are not random; you are the masterpiece of God's creation.

When you got saved, you were not only reconciled to God, you were also redefined. As a new creation in Christ, you became a partaker of divine nature (2 Peter 1:4). You now carry God's DNA, His uniqueness, and His supernatural essence.

You are not a mistake. You are God's intentional design, handcrafted by the Father, the Son, and the Holy Spirit. You are not defined by your past, your weaknesses, or your parents' choices. You are a product of Christ's resurrection and victory.

This supernatural identity confers divine abilities and privileges upon you. Stop measuring yourself by society's standards, your achievements, or your failures. Your true worth is found in God's narrative, not the world's opinion.

Many are searching for significance, unaware that their identity in God holds the key. Are you searching? You will find it in a real relationship with Him.

Quote of the Day: Stop measuring yourself by society's standards, your achievements, or your failures. Your true worth is found in God's narrative, not the world's opinion.

PERSONAL RESPONSE:

1. Do you truly see yourself the way God sees you?
2. What worldly definitions or personal experiences have wrongly shaped your sense of identity?
3. How can you begin to align your thoughts and actions with the supernatural identity God has given you?

Daily Prayer: Heavenly Father, thank You for creating me in Your image and redeeming me through Christ. Help me to see myself through Your eyes and walk boldly in the supernatural identity You have given me. Let my life reflect Your nature and purpose every day. In Jesus' name, amen.

Read the Bible in One Year: Psalms 126-128

SUPERNATURAL ENCOUNTERS

"Then Jacob was left alone, and a Man wrestled with him until the breaking of the day." Genesis 32:24

Do you know that your walk with God is meant to be an adventure filled with supernatural encounters? The Bible is a record of men and women whose lives were transformed, and who transformed their generation, through life-changing encounters with God.

What is an encounter? An encounter is when humanity interfaces with the supernatural; when you come face to face with the reality of God. You cannot claim to have encountered God if He has not become real to you. Genuine encounters leave a visible mark of God's glory on your life, just like they did on Moses. Encounters make God tangible in you and through you.

Everyone needs encounters. It begins with a sinner encountering Jesus, and continues with believers seeking deeper encounters with the power of God. It may be a drunk desperate for deliverance or a pastor seeking grace to heal the sick. Without encounters, the Christian life becomes dry and mechanical.

Jacob's story teaches us that desperation is a key ingredient for divine encounters. The Bible says he was left alone and wrestled with God until daybreak. He cried, "I will not let You go unless You bless me!" (Genesis 32:26). True hunger and thirst for God are what bring encounters that change destinies.

Do you need a supernatural encounter? Cry out to God today. Your life will always reflect the depth of your encounters with Him. No one ever truly met God and remained the same.

Quote of the Day: True hunger and thirst for God are what bring encounters that change destinies.

PERSONAL RESPONSE:

1. Have you ever had a personal, life-changing encounter with God, or has your walk with Him been mostly routine?
2. In what areas of your life are you currently desperate for a supernatural shift or breakthrough?
3. What can you begin doing today to cultivate the hunger and focus needed for deeper encounters with God?

Daily Prayer: Dear Lord, I do not want to live a dry and ordinary Christian life. Stir in me a holy desperation and hunger for You. I cry out for a fresh supernatural encounter that will transform me and align me fully with Your purpose for my life. In Jesus' name, amen.

Read the Bible in One Year: Psalms 129-131; 1 Corinthians 11

WORKING WITH ANGELS

"Are they not all ministering spirits sent forth to minister for those who will inherit salvation?" Hebrews 1:14

Angels are real spirit beings sent by God to help believers. Though assigned to minister to us, they often remain inactive until they are intentionally engaged. For example, an angel came to give Daniel understanding. An angel brought the good news to Mary (Luke 1:26–28). Angels destroyed Sodom and Gomorrah (Genesis 19). Angels also ministered to Jesus in the wilderness (Matthew 4:11).

These accounts show how important the ministry of angels is in a believer's life. Angels are activated when you pray. That is why every believer must cultivate a strong prayer life to fully benefit from their ministry. Praying with faith in your heart sets them in motion to carry out divine assignments.

God does not come down to do everything Himself; He delegates some tasks to angels. For instance, when the church prayed for Peter's release from prison, it was an angel who opened the prison doors (Acts 12:5–10). You must become conscious of the reality of angelic activity around you. Angels respond to your faith, your prayers, and your spoken words.

You do not need to be physically present at your child's school to protect them. You can release angels to watch over them. Angels also guard your home, possessions, and environment. They fight battles on your behalf.

May the Lord open your eyes today to understand the ministry of angels.

Quote of the Day: Angels are activated when you pray. That is why every believer must cultivate a strong prayer life to fully benefit from their ministry.

PERSONAL RESPONSE:

1. Are you consciously aware of the ministry of angels in your daily life, or have you neglected this supernatural provision?
2. How active is your prayer and faith life in engaging the help of angels as God intended?
3. In what areas of your life do you need to start declaring God's Word and releasing angelic assistance?

Daily Prayer: Father, thank You for assigning angels to minister to me. Open my eyes to their presence and teach me to engage them through faith-filled prayers and declarations. May I never take for granted the help You have made available through their ministry. In Jesus' name, amen.

Read the Bible in One Year: Psalms 132-134

CREATING AN ATMOSPHERE FOR THE SUPERNATURAL

"And the fire upon the altar shall be burning in it; it shall not be put out: and the priest shall burn wood on it every morning, and lay the burnt offering in order upon it, and he shall burn thereon the fat of the peace offerings." Leviticus 6:12

There is a specific atmosphere required for the supernatural to manifest. This is because the manifest presence of God does not appear just anywhere; it responds to certain conditions.

In our memory verse above, God instructed the priests to ensure that the fire on the altar never goes out. This was not just a physical act; it symbolized the spiritual responsibility of keeping the flame of devotion alive. God was teaching them that continuous fire is the key to experiencing His supernatural presence.

Likewise, in your life, there is an atmosphere you must create to host the supernatural power of God. One key way is through the mystery of praise and worship. When you consistently engage in heartfelt worship, the supernatural begins to flood your heart. You will start to experience the radiance of God's glory. God delights in worship. Wherever true worship is offered, His overflowing presence is released. If you desire to walk in different dimensions of the supernatural, you must become a passionate worshiper.

Finally, a heart saturated with the Word of God is a fertile ground for supernatural manifestations. God's presence always abides where His Word is welcomed and honoured. How much of God's Word do you carry in your heart? That is a question only you can answer.

Quote of the Day: There is a specific atmosphere required for the supernatural to manifest. This is because the manifest presence of God does not appear just anywhere; it responds to certain conditions.

PERSONAL RESPONSE:

1. Is the fire of devotion and worship burning continually on the altar of your heart, or has it grown cold?
2. How intentional are you about creating an atmosphere of praise, worship, and the Word in your daily life?
3. In what specific ways can you cultivate God's presence more consistently in your home, heart, or routine?

Daily Prayer: Dear Lord, help me to keep the fire on the altar of my heart burning daily. Teach me to live a life of worship, immerse myself in Your Word, and create an atmosphere that welcomes Your supernatural presence. Let my life be a dwelling place for Your glory. In Jesus' name, amen.

Read the Bible in One Year: Psalms 135-136; 1 Corinthians 12

SUPERNATURAL PEACE

"And the peace of God, which surpasses all understanding, will guard your hearts and minds through Christ Jesus." Philippians 4:7

Have you been trusting God for the blessing of supernatural peace? What does it really mean to experience such peace?

God desires that all His children walk in supernatural peace. He is not only the God of peace but also the Prince of Peace. Supernatural peace is His promise to you. It would be a tragedy to constantly live in anxiety and storms when you have access to the peace of God.

So, what is the secret to this kind of peace? The Apostle Paul told the Philippians that the key to experiencing supernatural peace is living in an atmosphere of thanksgiving. A heart that praises will always enjoy peace.

Another secret is refusing to live in anxiety or worry. When you learn to cast your cares on God, His peace will flood your soul. Anxiety steals your joy, and where joy is absent, peace cannot dwell.

Additionally, Scripture teaches that to experience supernatural peace, your mind must be fixed on God. Your thoughts must be pure. You must make a conscious decision to reject negative thinking. The fruit of negativity is fear, and where fear reigns, peace cannot thrive.

There you have it: the secrets to living in the supernatural peace God has promised.

Quote of the Day: The key to experiencing supernatural peace is living in an atmosphere of thanksgiving. A heart that praises will always enjoy peace.

PERSONAL RESPONSE:

1. Are there areas of your life where anxiety has replaced thanksgiving and trust in God?
2. What practical steps can you take to cultivate a mindset that is fixed on God and free from negative thoughts?
3. How often do you intentionally thank and praise God, even when circumstances seem uncertain?

Daily Prayer: Heavenly Father, I surrender every anxious thought and burden to You. Fill my heart and mind with Your supernatural peace. Teach me to live in constant thanksgiving, keep my mind pure, and trust You fully so that Your peace may guard my life every day. In Jesus' name, amen.

Read the Bible in One Year: Psalms 137-139; 1 Corinthians 13

HOW TO ACTIVATE THE SUPERNATURAL

"By which have been given to us exceedingly great and precious promises, that through these you may be partakers of the divine nature, having escaped the corruption that is in the world through lust." 2 Peter 1:4

Do you desire to live in an atmosphere where your daily experiences reflect the supernatural? If so, then it is important to pay attention to today's devotional.

First, understand that the supernatural refers to anything that transcends the natural. While the human spirit can accomplish much, a person who learns to tap into the supernatural will live an extraordinary life. You will operate under open heavens, and your reality will differ from the ordinary.

So, how can you activate the supernatural in your life? It begins with understanding that you have a divine nature. As a partaker of God's nature, you carry the potential to walk in His supernatural power.

Here are three key ways to activate it:

- **Live a life of ardent faith.** The woman with the issue of blood tapped into the supernatural healing power of God through faith.
- **Walk in obedience to divine instruction.** Abraham's life was filled with supernatural encounters because he obeyed God completely.
- **Be devoted to prayer.** Prayer activates divine resources. It's the channel through which God's supernatural power is released.

Do you long to activate the supernatural in your life? Then spend time praying in the Spirit daily. That is a potent way to connect with the power of heaven.

Quote of the Day: While the human spirit can accomplish much, a person who learns to tap into the supernatural will live an extraordinary life.

PERSONAL RESPONSE QUESTIONS

1. Have you fully embraced your identity as a partaker of God's divine nature, or are you still living with a limited, natural mindset?
2. Which of the three keys discussed in today's devotional do you need to strengthen most in your life right now to activate the supernatural?
3. Are you consistent in praying in the Spirit, or have you neglected this vital channel of supernatural power?

Daily Prayer: Father, thank You for making me a partaker of Your divine nature. Help me to walk daily in faith, obedience, and fervent prayer. Teach me to live under open heavens and activate Your supernatural power in every area of my life. In Jesus' name, amen.

Read the Bible in One Year: Psalms 140-142

DECEMBER 12

THE SUPERNATURAL WORK OF THE HOLY SPIRIT

> ***"But the Helper, the Holy Spirit, whom the Father will send in My name, He will teach you all things, and bring to your remembrance all things that I said to you." John 14:26***

One of the blessings that comes with the new birth is the outpouring of the Holy Spirit. The moment you gave your life to Christ, God poured out His Spirit into your life. The first supernatural work of the Holy Spirit is to **transform your mind**. He is the One responsible for the renewal, realignment, and transformation of your thoughts. Without His help, you cannot experience a true supernatural shift. This transformation only happens as you build a consistent life of **fellowship and intimacy** with the Holy Spirit.

Furthermore, the Holy Spirit **guides you into truth**, especially the truth of your identity and reality as a new creation in Christ. By His influence, you begin to grasp the depths of your inheritance in Christ.

Additionally, it is **through the supernatural work of the Holy Spirit** that you operate in miracles, healings, signs, and wonders. As you yield your life to Him, you begin to walk in the fullness of God's power and authority.

The Holy Spirit has been given to you so that you can live a supernatural life on Earth. As you grow in intimacy with Him, your experiences will begin to reflect the reality of heaven. Do you want to experience the supernatural naturally? Then align yourself fully with the Holy Spirit.

Quote of the Day: The Holy Spirit has been given to you so that you can live a supernatural life on Earth.

PERSONAL RESPONSE:

1. Are you actively building a life of intimacy and fellowship with the Holy Spirit, or have you neglected His presence in your daily walk?
2. In what ways has your mind been transformed since you received the Holy Spirit, and what areas still need His renewal?
3. Are you consciously yielding to the Holy Spirit so He can work miracles, reveal truth, and lead you into the fullness of your inheritance in Christ?

Daily Prayer: Holy Spirit, I yield my heart and life to You today. Transform my mind, guide me into all truth, and help me to walk in the power and authority of my identity in Christ. Let my life be a reflection of heaven on Earth as I live in step with You. In Jesus' name, amen.

Read the Bible in One Year: Psalms 143-145; 1 Corinthians 14

SUPERNATURAL SPEED

"And the hand of the LORD was on Elijah, and he girded up his loins and ran ahead of Ahab to the entrance of Jezreel." 1 Kings 18:46

Do you know that supernatural speed is both a reality and a possibility in God? In today's devotional, you will discover that God wants you, as His child, to walk in supernatural speed.

You need supernatural speed to **pursue, overtake, and recover** all that the enemy may have stolen from you, especially due to past ignorance or delays. Now that you are a new creation in Christ, it is important to understand that God desires for you to live a life empowered by divine acceleration.

What exactly is supernatural speed? The Bible gives us a striking example in the life of **Elijah**. After the contest on Mount Carmel, Elijah prayed earnestly for rain. When he saw the sign of its coming, he quickly informed King Ahab. Remarkably, Elijah outran the king's chariot all the way to Jezreel. This was not ordinary speed; it was **supernatural**.

It was **the hand of the Lord** upon Elijah that gave him the strength and acceleration to outrun horses and chariots. The hand of God represents His presence, and where His presence is, **power is released**.

Are you feeling delayed in life, business, marriage, or ministry? Cry out to God today. Ask for His hand to rest upon you, because when His hand comes, **supernatural speed follows**.

Quote of the Day: The hand of God represents His presence, and where His presence is, **power is released**.

PERSONAL RESPONSE:

1. In what area of your life do you currently feel delayed or stuck, and have you invited God into that situation?
2. Are you relying on your own strength or truly depending on the hand of the Lord to empower your progress?
3. What steps can you take today to position yourself for divine acceleration through prayer and obedience?

Daily Prayer: Father, I ask that Your hand would rest mightily upon me. Let every delay be turned into divine acceleration. Empower me by Your presence to pursue, overtake, and recover all that has been lost. Let supernatural speed become my testimony in every area of my life. In Jesus' name, amen.

Read the Bible in One Year: Psalms 146-147; 1 Corinthians 15

SUPERNATURAL FAVOUR

"Thou shalt arise, and have mercy upon Zion: for the time to favour her, yea, the set time, is come." Psalm 102:13

What is supernatural favour? How can you experience it? Throughout Scripture, we see examples of what it means to walk in God's favour. Concerning Jesus, the Bible says He grew in favour with both God and men. That same favour is available to you.

If God is going to do anything significant in a person's life, it begins with favour. When a man finds favour with God, it causes others to favour him too. Supernatural favour is what brings restoration of all that has been lost.

Consider **Joseph**, a young man destined for greatness. His coat of many colours was stained with betrayal and suffering. He spent 11 years in prison, but the day God showed him favour, everything changed. What he lost was not only restored; it was also multiplied.

Are you dealing with pain from past disappointments or broken dreams? The favour of God can turn your shame into glory and your mourning into dancing. When supernatural favour rests on you, like it did on Joseph, it brings supernatural **increase**, **promotion**, and **honour**, even in the midst of enemies. It sets you apart and releases uncommon blessings. A man favoured by God will not lack good things; he will flourish in prosperity.

God wants you to experience this dimension of favour. That is the reason for today's devotional. Be expectant. Get ready for an **avalanche of supernatural favour** in your life, family, business, and finances.

Quote of the Day: If God is going to do anything significant in a person's life, it begins with favour. When a man finds favour with God, it causes others to favour him too.

PERSONAL RESPONSE:

1. Have you been trying to succeed by effort alone, or are you trusting God to clothe you with His supernatural favour?
2. In what areas of your life do you most need God's favour to bring restoration and promotion?
3. How can you position your heart to walk in favour like Joseph?

Daily Prayer: Father, I thank You for the gift of supernatural favour. Let Your favour rest upon me and distinguish me in every area of my life. Restore all I have lost, promote me beyond human effort, and let my life become a testimony of Your mercy and goodness. In Jesus' name, amen.

Read the Bible in One Year: Psalms 148-150

SUPERNATURAL MIRACLES

***"For she said, 'If only I may touch His clothes, I shall be made well.'"* Mark 5:28**

Do you need a supernatural miracle in your life, family, finances, health, or ministry? God is not distant or indifferent to your needs. He is a loving Father who desires to intervene in your situation and display His power on your behalf.

God is intentional about you. He knows your frame and understands the deep cries of your heart. He sees your pain, your weariness, and the silent battles you fight. This devotional is a reminder that you are marked by God for a supernatural miracle.

The story of the woman with the issue of blood is a timeless illustration. She had suffered for twelve years, physically, financially, and socially. But one day, something shifted: her faith rose. She said to herself, *"If only I may touch His clothes, I shall be made well."* That inner conviction, coupled with action, brought healing.

Her faith broke through every obstacle: fear, shame, and the crowd. And when she touched Jesus in faith, power flowed.

Do you want to see such miracles in your own life? Walk in unshakable faith. Declare God's promises boldly. Refuse to doubt. Miracles do not respond to need. They respond to faith. Touch Him today with your faith, and watch heaven move on your behalf.

Quote of the Day: Miracles do not respond to need. They respond to faith.

PERSONAL RESPONSE:

1. Are you exercising bold, unshakable faith in the areas where you need a miracle, or have you allowed doubt to take root?
2. What is currently standing in the way of your desperation for a miracle?
3. How often do you actively confess and declare God's promises over your circumstances in faith?

Daily Prayer: Lord Jesus, I believe that You are the God of miracles. Strengthen my faith and teach me to stand on Your promises without wavering. Let my heart burn with fresh desperation for Your touch, and may supernatural miracles break forth in every area of my life as I put my trust in You. In your very dear name, I pray. Amen.

Read the Bible in One Year: Proverbs 1-2; 1 Corinthians 16

DECEMBER 16

THE SUPERNATURAL CHURCH MEMBER

"But without faith it is impossible to please Him, for he who comes to God must believe that He is, and that He is a rewarder of those who diligently seek Him." Hebrews 11:6

God is a supernatural being, far above the natural, beyond the ordinary, and superior to all that is mundane. If there were a stronger word to describe God's supremacy over the natural realm, it would still fall short. He is infinite, eternal, and all-powerful.

Now, some people assume that such a supernatural God must reside in some distant, mystical place. This has led many to seek Him through various religions and philosophies. Yet the truth remains: as God is supernatural, so are His offspring. **Glory!** We are not just children of God; we are *supernatural* **children of God**. We are not just church attendees; we are partakers of divine nature with access to God's supernatural provisions **through faith**. That Is why, whenever we approach God's presence, we must first believe that **He is**, and that **He rewards those who diligently seek Him**. God will manifest Himself in any area where you diligently pursue Him. You have access to dimensions in God beyond the natural. The more aware you are of this truth, the more you will walk in it. Philip is an example of a supernatural church member. He expounded the Scriptures to the Ethiopian eunuch and was later supernaturally transported. That is not fiction; it is the reality of one who walked with God. Today, God invites you to go deeper. Do not be an ordinary church member. Be on fire. Be intentional. Soak in the consciousness of who you are and bring **evidence** of God's Word to life.

Quote of the Day: Do not be an ordinary church member. Be on fire. Be intentional. Soak in the consciousness of who you are and bring **evidence** of God's Word to life.

PERSONAL RESPONSE:

1. In what specific ways have you been limiting your walk with God to the natural, instead of embracing your supernatural identity as His child?
2. How conscious are you of the supernatural dimensions available to you as a believer, and how often do you intentionally press into them by faith?
3. Like Philip, are you living in a way that proves the reality and power of the Word you profess to believe and share?

Daily Prayer: Father, awaken in me the consciousness of who I truly am in You. Help me to live daily as a supernatural church member, full of faith, walking in Your power, and bringing visible evidence of Your Word. Let my life reflect the reality of heaven on earth. In Jesus' name, Amen.

Read the Bible in One Year: Proverbs 3-5; 2 Corinthians 1

THE SUPERNATURAL POWER OF JOY

"Then [Ezra] told them, 'Go your way, eat the fat, drink the sweet drink, and send portions to him for whom nothing is prepared; for this day is holy to our Lord. And do not be grieved and depressed, for the joy of the Lord is your strength and stronghold.'" Nehemiah 8:10

Why are you wallowing in self-pity? Why are you sinking into distress? Why do you keep giving room for the devil to toss you around on the waves of depression?

Let us consider the story of the Israelites and the wall of Jericho. It was time for them to possess the Promised Land, but a mighty obstacle stood in their way. How could a great fortified wall be brought down so a whole nation could move forward?

Then, God unveiled a weapon: **Joy.** The Lord commanded them to rejoice, to march, shout, and praise. It seemed foolish to dance and sing in the face of such a massive obstacle, but God's ways are not man's ways. At the sound of their joyful praise, the wall of Jericho collapsed like a pack of cards. That is how your own strongholds are shattered when you engage the supernatural tool of **joy**.

Are you weak? Do you feel overwhelmed? The joy of the Lord is your **strength**. Only through joy can you draw from the wells of salvation (Isaiah 12:3). The supernatural thrives in an atmosphere of joy.

So, rise up! Rejoice and glorify the One who called you out of darkness. Victory, strength, and breakthrough await you , but they come through joy. **Be joyful and rejoice today, for joy is your weapon.**

Quote of the Day: The supernatural thrives in an atmosphere of joy.

PERSONAL RESPONSE:

1. How often do you intentionally choose joy when facing challenges, or do you find yourself defaulting to self-pity and discouragement?
2. What "walls of Jericho" are currently standing in your life, and how can you begin to confront them through joyful praise?
3. In what ways have you underestimated the power of joy as a spiritual weapon in your walk with God?

Daily Prayer: Father, thank You for the gift of supernatural joy. Help me to rise above discouragement and fear by anchoring my heart in the joy of the Lord. Let Your joy become my strength, and may praise continually erupt from my heart until every wall before me collapses, in Jesus' name. Amen.

Read the Bible in One Year: Proverbs 6-7; 2 Corinthians 2

THERE IS ALWAYS MORE

"But the path of the just is like the shining sun, that shines ever brighter unto the perfect day." Proverbs 4:18

The moment you become comfortable in your walk with God, beware, you may be under spiritual attack. As believers, we are called to shine *brighter and brighter* until the perfect day. There is always more in God.

In Ezekiel 47, the prophet describes a vision revealing dimensions of the supernatural. There was water at ankle-deep, knee-deep, waist-deep, and finally, water deep enough to swim in, an overflowing dimension. I do not know about you, but I want to get to that overflowing level.

The supernatural becomes natural to those who *hunger* for more of God. No matter how much of Him you have experienced, there is still more. Like Paul, you must forget what lies behind and press on toward higher dimensions of God's power and presence.

Have you seen blind eyes open? There is still power to raise the dead. Have you seen souls saved? You can also see them transformed. Never get emotionally attached to your past achievements with God. Keep looking upward. As the saying goes, "Yesterday's win is often tomorrow's hindrance."

There are more mysteries in God yet to be discovered. Do not settle. Do not park here. Do you want to gain new heights in God? Seek the deeper things of the Kingdom. **There is always more.**

Quote of the Day: Never get emotionally attached to your past achievements with God. Keep looking upward.

PERSONAL RESPONSE:

1. Are you currently coasting in your spiritual life, or are you actively pressing into deeper dimensions of God?
2. What past achievements or experiences with God might be keeping you from seeking "the more" He has for you?
3. What intentional steps can you take today to pursue a greater level of intimacy and supernatural experience with God?

Daily Prayer: Heavenly Father, I thank You for what You have done in my life so far, but I refuse to settle. Stir in me a holy hunger for more of You. Take me deeper, Lord, into overflowing waters, greater power, and deeper intimacy with Your Spirit. I press forward, leaving the past behind, that I may walk in all You have destined for me. In Jesus' name, Amen.

Read the Bible in One Year: Proverbs 8-9; 2 Corinthians 3

LET THE SUPERNATURAL WORK FOR YOU

"Now unto him that is able to do exceeding abundantly above all that we ask or think, according to the power that worketh in us." Ephesians 3:20

God is a supernatural being, and with Him, there are no limitations to the possibilities available to you. By divine provision, God can grant you access to jobs, contracts, business opportunities, and ideas you may not even be qualified for by human standards. The supernatural hand of God can go ahead of you into a job interview and stir the hearts of decision-makers to grant you favour, even before you speak a word.

As long as you are a child of God, His favour will speak for you. You must learn to engage the supernatural help and favour of God whenever you face important tasks or critical moments in your life.

If promotions and positions were based strictly on qualifications, David would not have become king of Israel. Likewise, Joseph had no formal credentials to become prime minister in a foreign land, but God's supernatural favour lifted him.

While diligence and excellence in your work are important, you must also allow the supernatural hand of God to flow into your labour. When you yield your work to God, His influence begins to manifest through it.

Are you currently facing challenges in your career or business? Be assured that God is faithful. He will supply all you need in due time. Trust Him. Rely on Him. Let His power be seen in your work, and watch the supernatural become your reality.

Quote of the Day: As long as you are a child of God, His favour will speak for you. You must learn to engage the supernatural help and favour of God whenever you face important tasks or critical moments in your life.

PERSONAL RESPONSE:

1. In what areas of your life have you been relying solely on your qualifications instead of trusting in God's supernatural help?
2. How can you begin to invite God's presence into your daily work or business decisions?
3. Have you limited your expectations based on what you think you deserve? What would it look like to expect "exceedingly abundantly" from God?

Daily Prayer: Father, I surrender my work, plans, and ambitions to You. Let Your supernatural favour go ahead of me and open doors that no man can shut. Help me to rely on Your power, not just my efforts, and cause my work to reflect Your glory. In Jesus' name, Amen.

Read the Bible in One Year: Proverbs 10-12; 2 Corinthians 4

THE SUPERNATURAL POWER OF AGREEMENT

"Again I say to you that if two of you agree concerning anything they ask, it will be done for them by My Father in heaven." Matthew 18:19

To agree means to align, consent, and harmonize over a matter. Have you ever heard a choir sing in perfect harmony? The result is beautiful because unity creates power.

Psalm 133:1 says, *"Behold, how good and how pleasant it is for brethren to dwell together in unity."* Agreement births a supernatural atmosphere that invites divine intervention. Some breakthroughs will only come in the place of corporate agreement.

Jesus emphasized this: when two people come together in agreement and ask according to His will, heaven responds. So do not suffer in silence when faced with overwhelming situations. Find a mature believer, your spouse, or a spiritual friend, and engage in the prayer of agreement.

You might wonder, *"How do I know I'm praying God's will?"* Simply check if your request aligns with the Word of God. If it does, then your answer is near. For example, Psalm 113:9 says that God gives the barren woman a home and makes her a joyful mother. That is His will. If your request aligns with such a promise, join hands with another believer and pray in faith.

Today, I pray for you: may your desires, as long as they are within God's will, be granted. Your miracle is on the way, by the power of agreement.

Quote of the Day: Agreement births a supernatural atmosphere that invites divine intervention.

PERSONAL RESPONSE:

1. Are there situations in your life right now where you have been trying to go it alone instead of seeking the supernatural power of agreement in prayer?
2. Do you have someone in your life with whom you can regularly engage in the prayer of agreement?
3. Are your current prayer requests aligned with the clear promises in God's Word, or are there areas where you need to search the Scriptures for confirmation?

Daily Prayer: Father, I thank You for the gift of agreement in prayer. Today, I ask for discernment to recognize Your will, the humility to invite others into my faith journey, and the grace to pray in unity for breakthroughs that reflect Your promises. Let heaven respond swiftly to every prayer I make in alignment with Your Word. In Jesus' name, amen.

Read the Bible in One Year: Proverbs 13-15; 2 Corinthians 5

SUPERNATURAL GIFTS

"Every good gift and every perfect gift is from above, and comes down from the Father of lights, with whom there is no variation or shadow of turning." James 1:17

Every person on earth is gifted, but more importantly, everyone who has accepted Jesus as Lord and Saviour is supernaturally gifted. That is partly what sets a saved person apart from the unsaved.

God does not create failures. In every person, He has deposited potential. You must begin to see yourself as a supernatural being with extraordinary talents and divine purpose.

What is a gift? It is something freely given. Likewise, the supernatural gifts of God in your life are given freely. But until you realize this, you may live feeling empty, even though you are full of value.

Remember the parable of the talents. Each servant was given something, at least one talent. That means **you too have been given something by God.** But it is not enough to merely know that you are gifted. You must discover that gift and develop it. Your gift is what God will use to make room for you in life (Proverbs 18:16).

Finally, every gift must be used. When you use the supernatural gifts God has given you, He is glorified. You are not just gifted; your gifts are supernatural because they come from above. And everything from above surpasses the natural.

Quote of the Day: It is not enough to merely know that you are gifted. You must discover that gift and develop it.

PERSONAL RESPONSE:

1. Have you taken time to discover the supernatural gift God has placed in you?
2. In what specific ways are you currently using your God-given gifts to glorify Him and bless others?
3. Are there fears, excuses, or distractions that are stopping you from developing or using your gift?

Daily Prayer: Heavenly Father, thank You for the supernatural gifts You have deposited in me. Open my eyes to see what You have placed inside me, stir my heart to develop it, and give me the courage and wisdom to use it for Your glory. Let my life reflect the excellence of Your workmanship in Jesus' name. Amen.

Read the Bible in One Year: Proverbs 16-18; 2 Corinthians 6

DECEMBER 22

SUPERNATURAL ABILITY

"I can do all things through Christ who strengthens me." Philippians 4:13

You can become everything God created you to be. But you must first believe it. The only person who can stop you from fulfilling your God-ordained destiny is *you*. Too often, we magnify the devil and underestimate the supernatural ability God has placed within us.

Do you realize you are fighting an enemy who has already been defeated? It is a contradiction for you, as a child of God, to live a defeated life when you have access to divine strength. You are a supernatural being, and the power to walk in victory is already inside you.

The Bible says, *"I can do all things"*, but the secret lies in the next part: *"through Christ who strengthens me."* Anything done outside Christ is not His will, and He is not committed to supporting it.

Strive always to know His will. Once you do, trust Him completely. God never assigns a task without first equipping you for it. He deposits the strength you need within you beforehand.

Remember, you live in a realm of divine possibilities because Christ lives in you. Embrace this supernatural empowerment and watch God do through you what others consider impossible.

Today, walk in the boldness of your identity in Christ. You are supernaturally empowered!

Quote of the Day: God never assigns a task without first equipping you for it.

PERSONAL RESPONSE:

1. Are you living with the daily consciousness that God has supernaturally empowered you to fulfil His purpose?
2. What limiting beliefs or fears have you allowed to hinder your confidence in God's strength within you?
3. How often do you seek God's will before acting, and are you willing to trust His ability in you above your own limitations?

Daily Prayer: Lord, I thank You for the supernatural strength You have placed within me through Christ. Help me to walk in the full awareness of this power, trusting Your ability in me to do all You have called me to do. In Jesus' name, Amen.

Read the Bible in One Year: Proverbs 19-21; 2 Corinthians 7

SUPERNATURAL ACCESS

"Let us therefore come boldly to the throne of grace, that we may obtain mercy and find grace to help in time of need." Hebrews 4:16

The greatest gift every man in Christ has received is the gift of access into God's presence and every divine possibility available in Him. Through the blood of Jesus, you now have unhindered, direct access to the Father. No more walls of guilt, fear, or condemnation. You can come boldly before God, not as a beggar, but as a beloved child. As Paul rightly declares in *Ephesians 2:18, "For through Him we both have access by one Spirit to the Father."*

It is not enough to merely know that Jesus died for you. You must also understand what His sacrifice has secured for you. You have access to the peace that passes understanding, the joy that overflows, healing for your body, wisdom for your decisions, strength in your trials, and dominion over every force of darkness. You are no longer a stranger to the covenant of promise. You are now a citizen of heaven, with full rights and privileges in Christ.

However, this access is not passive. It must be engaged. Boldness is the key. Come before God with confidence, knowing that the blood of Jesus is your guaranteed access.

Live today with the awareness that you have supernatural access. Through that access, your life will shine, and nations will be drawn to your light.

Quote of the Day: It is not enough to merely know that Jesus died for you. You must also understand what His sacrifice has secured for you.

PERSONAL RESPONSE:

1. Do you truly believe that the blood of Jesus gives you full access to God's presence, or do you still approach Him with fear and guilt?
2. In what areas of your life have you failed to take advantage of the supernatural access you have in Christ?
3. How can you begin to walk more boldly in prayer, faith, and purpose, knowing that you are no longer a stranger to God's promises?

Daily Prayer: Father, I thank You for the access I have to You through the blood of Jesus. Today, I boldly enter into Your presence. Let me walk daily in the fullness of my inheritance, accessing Your peace, power, and provision without fear or shame. In Jesus' name, amen.

Read the Bible in One Year: Proverbs 22-24; 2 Corinthians 8

DECEMBER 24

SUPERNATURAL HEALTH

> *"And Jesus went about all Galilee, teaching in their synagogues, preaching the gospel of the kingdom, and healing all kinds of sickness and all kinds of disease among the people." Matthew 4:23*

Do you know that God's will for you is divine health? He has blessed you with abundance and prosperity, and He wants you to enjoy supernatural health as part of that blessing.

We see God's supernatural ability to give divine health in how He preserved the Israelites in the wilderness for 40 years. Despite harsh conditions, their health did not fail. Their strength was sustained supernaturally. More so, Jesus is the embodiment of all the goodness of God to mankind. He did not just come to save or teach; He also came to heal. The Bible says He went about healing *all* kinds of sickness and disease (Matthew 4:23). Jesus left no need unattended in His earthly ministry.

It is God's desire for you to be in health, not just in your body, but in every area of your life. However, what you believe is what you receive. If you believe in God's healing power, then you can receive it by faith. Just like Naaman received healing by obeying prophetic instruction, you too can walk in supernatural health by trusting God's Word.

Are you constantly visiting the hospital? Do you feel worn out or afflicted? Now is the time to tell the devil to take his hands off your body and life. Speak healing over your body, your business, your relationships, and your finances. Declare God's Word boldly. By His stripes, you are healed.

Quote of the Day: It is God's desire for you to be in health, not just in your body, but in every area of your life. However, what you believe is what you receive. If you believe in God's healing power, then you can receive it by faith.

PERSONAL RESPONSE:

1. Do you truly believe that divine health is part of your inheritance in Christ, or are you tolerating certain afflictions as normal?
2. What areas of your life need the touch of God's healing power today?
3. Are you consistently speaking and standing on God's Word concerning your health and well-being?

Daily Prayer: Father, I thank You for making divine health my portion through Christ. I declare that every area of my life aligns with Your supernatural power. I receive healing, strength, and vitality, in Jesus' name. Amen.

Read the Bible in One Year: Proverbs 25-26; 2 Corinthians 9

THE SUPERNATURAL POWER OF THANKSGIVING

"Let the peoples praise You, O God; let all the peoples praise You. Then the earth shall yield her increase; God, our own God, shall bless us." Psalms 67:5-6

David was the one who introduced us to the principle that access to God begins with thanksgiving. If you desire to experience God's presence, favour, and abundance, the entry point is a grateful heart. Thanksgiving is not just a polite gesture; it is a powerful spiritual key that unlocks supernatural dimensions of God's blessings.

You can give God your money. You can give Him your heart. And you can also give Him thanks. That, too, is a precious gift. Are you searching for something to offer God today? Start with gratitude. Thank Him for the victories you know about and the ones He won for you behind the scenes. Thank Him for watching over you when you were unaware. Thank Him for your family, your health, and your daily provisions.

Thank Him for where He brought you from, where you are now, and where He is taking you. Thanksgiving provokes supernatural increase. Just like Jesus gave thanks and five loaves and two fish fed thousands (John 6:11), your thanksgiving can multiply God's seed in your life.

Do you want to enjoy divine favour and breakthrough? Then immerse yourself in the practice of thanksgiving. Grumbling drives God away, but thanksgiving draws Him near. Every time you give thanks, you make room for more. Choose gratitude today, and watch heaven respond. Hallelujah!

Quote of the Day: Grumbling drives God away, but thanksgiving draws Him near.

PERSONAL RESPONSE:

1. In what areas of your life have you allowed complaints and grumbling to replace thanksgiving?
2. What are three specific things God has done for you that you haven't properly thanked Him for?
3. How can you intentionally cultivate a daily habit of thanksgiving regardless of your circumstances?

Daily Prayer: Father, thank You for all You have done in my life, seen and unseen. Today, I choose to give You thanks in all things. Teach me to live with a grateful heart that draws Your presence and multiplies Your blessings in my life. In Jesus' name, amen.

Read the Bible in One Year: Proverbs 27-29; 2 Corinthians 10

SUPERNATURAL WISDOM

"As for these four young men, God gave them knowledge and skill in all literature and wisdom; and Daniel had understanding in all visions and dreams." Daniel 1:17

Every child of God has been endowed with supernatural wisdom. This is what sets you apart from the children of the world.

The supernatural wisdom that comes from God cannot be taught or learned in a classroom. It is imparted through the gift of the Holy Spirit. As a believer, you have access to this divine intelligence. When it begins to operate in your life, it brings you favour before God and men. It unlocks insights, ideas, and strategies that can bring lasting solutions to complex problems. It distinguishes you among your peers and sets you on a path of excellence.

Supernatural wisdom is your covenant advantage. When you walk in it, you begin to operate in different dimensions of God's possibilities. This same wisdom was present at creation. It is God's operating system. That means you carry within you the potential to birth creative and innovative ideas that can redefine your world.

You must pray earnestly for this grace to manifest fully in your life. The more you engage the wisdom of God, the more naturally you will walk in the supernatural. This wisdom transforms ordinary people into extraordinary vessels.

Daniel walked in this wisdom, and it changed his destiny. Do you want to transform your life, family, ministry, or nation? Supernatural wisdom is your divine advantage. You must contend for it if you want to do great exploits.

Quote of the Day: The supernatural wisdom that comes from God cannot be taught or learned in a classroom. It is imparted through the gift of the Holy Spirit.

PERSONAL RESPONSE:

1. In what areas of your life do you most need supernatural wisdom right now?
2. How intentional are you about praying for and cultivating divine insight through the Holy Spirit?
3. What practical steps can you take this week to rely less on human reasoning and more on God's wisdom?

Daily Prayer: Heavenly Father, I thank You for the gift of supernatural wisdom made available through Your Spirit. Today, I ask that You open my mind and heart to receive this divine wisdom that will set me apart. Fill me with insight that brings solutions, favour, and exploits for Your glory. Let Your wisdom be my daily guide, in Jesus' name. Amen.

Read the Bible in One Year: Proverbs 30-31; 2 Corinthians 11

THE SUPERNATURAL POWER OF LOVE

"Therefore the sisters sent to Him, saying, 'Lord, behold, he whom You love is sick.'" John 11:3

One consistent pattern in the earthly ministry of Jesus was this: every miracle He performed was rooted in love and compassion. Whether He was feeding the multitudes, healing the sick, or raising the dead, love was always the foundation, demonstrating to us that love is a trigger of the supernatural. Wherever love thrives, miracles follow. Love creates an atmosphere where the supernatural can flow unhindered.

Take, for example, the story of Lazarus in John 11:1–44. The Bible tells us that when Jesus saw the grief of Mary and Martha, He was deeply moved, and He wept (John 11:35). His love for Lazarus stirred Him to action. That same love is alive today. Jesus still weeps with you, walks with you, and is eager to show Himself strong on your behalf.

If you are trusting God for a miracle, begin by resting in the assurance of His love. The revelation of God as a loving Father unlocks faith, and faith is the doorway to the miraculous. And if you want God to perform miracles *through* you, then become a vessel of love. Let your heart be tender, your spirit compassionate, and your life surrendered. Love opens the floodgates of heaven.

PERSONAL RESPONSE:

1. Do you truly believe that God loves you and desires to work miracles in your life?
2. In what ways can you cultivate a more compassionate heart that reflects the love of Christ?
3. Are there areas in your life where love is lacking, and could that be hindering the flow of the supernatural?

Daily Prayer: Father, help me to rest in the assurance of Your love. Fill my heart with genuine compassion so that I may become a vessel through which Your miraculous power flows. Let love rule in me, and let Your power be revealed through me. In Jesus' name, Amen.

Read the Bible in One Year: Ecclesiastes 1-3

SUPERNATURAL BREAKTHROUGH

"And David came to Baal-perazim, and David defeated them there. And he said, 'The Lord has burst through my enemies before me like a bursting flood.' Therefore the name of that place is called Baal-perazim." 2 Samuel 5:20

God wants to give you a supernatural breakthrough. He is deeply invested in every detail of your life and desires to see you walk in consistent victory. There is no mountain too high or battle too fierce that God cannot overcome on your behalf. You belong to a victorious God, and it is not His will for you to remain under the yoke and oppression of the enemy.

However, divine breakthroughs require your cooperation. You cannot live outside of God's plans and purposes and still expect supernatural results. Victory comes when you align with His will.

Could it be that the delay or opposition you are facing today is a result of disobedience to God's instructions? Now is the time to return to God with humility and ask for mercy. His arms are open to restore you.

Scripture tells us how God broke through the seemingly impossible barrier of Abraham and Sarah's barrenness. Their breakthrough came through faith and obedience. The same principle applies today.

If you are longing for a supernatural breakthrough, begin by obeying every instruction God gives you. Respond in faith, even when it does not make sense. As you do, get ready: your breakthrough is not only possible, it is near. **Believe, obey, and be expectant.**

Quote of the Day: You cannot live outside of God's plans and purposes and still expect supernatural results. Victory comes when you align with His will.

PERSONAL RESPONSE:

1. Are there any specific instructions from God that you have been reluctant to obey, and could that be delaying your breakthrough?
2. In what ways have you tried to fight your battles alone instead of partnering with God through faith and obedience?
3. What steps can you begin to take today to realign your life with God's plans and position yourself for supernatural breakthrough?

Daily Prayer: Dear Lord, I surrender every area of my life to You. Where I have walked in disobedience, forgive me. Give me the grace to obey Your voice completely and the faith to believe You for the impossible. Let every delayed breakthrough be released as I align with Your will. In Jesus' name, amen.

Read the Bible in One Year: Ecclesiastes 4-6; 2 Corinthians 12

PARTNERING WITH GOD FOR THE SUPERNATURAL

"For we are labourers together with God: ye are God's husbandry, ye are God's building." 1 Corinthians 3:9

Do you know that the Christian life is designed to be a supernatural life? Yet today, many believers live far below this reality. Their daily experiences do not reflect the supernatural life that God intended.

God desires that you walk in the supernatural every single day, not just when a guest minister visits your church or when you attend a special service. Have you forgotten that Scripture clearly states you are a man or woman of God? You carry His Spirit within you!

So why do many believers fall short of this experience? One major reason is that they try to achieve spiritual results on their own. But the supernatural life is never meant to be lived independently. It is sustained through partnership with God.

From Noah to Daniel, from Elijah to Elisha, and ultimately Jesus Himself, all those who lived in the realm of the supernatural had one thing in common: they walked in deep communion with God. Their power came from partnership, especially through fervent, prevailing prayer.

Today, God is extending that same invitation to you. He wants to work with you. He is calling you into His secret place. It is time to activate your prayer altar and engage heaven. Receive grace now for the spirit of prayer and supplication.

Quote of the Day: The supernatural life is never meant to be lived independently. It is sustained through partnership with God.

PERSONAL RESPONSE:

1. Are you currently trying to live the Christian life in your own strength, or are you actively partnering with God in prayer?
2. How consistent and intentional are you in cultivating a lifestyle of communion with God through fervent prayer?
3. What changes do you need to make in your daily routine to deepen your partnership with God and walk in the supernatural?

Daily Prayer: Father, I receive grace today for a deeper walk with You. Stir in me the spirit of prayer and supplication. Help me to partner with You daily, so that the supernatural becomes my natural experience, in Jesus' name. Amen.

Read the Bible in One Year: Ecclesiastes 7-9; 2 Corinthians 13

SUPERNATURAL ABUNDANCE

"And God is able to provide you with every blessing in abundance, so that you may always have enough of everything and may provide in abundance for every good work." 2 Corinthians 9:8

To walk in supernatural abundance means to enjoy limitless divine provision and overflowing grace. The truth is, everything made by man eventually comes to an end, but God's supernatural abundance is endless.

From the very beginning, God spoke abundance into existence. He commanded the seas, skies, and land to abound with life, and everything began to multiply on its own accord (Genesis 1:20–28). Likewise, the regenerated human spirit in Christ has been designed to abound. You are wired for all-round abundance, spiritually, emotionally, financially, mentally, socially, and materially. The divine life we have received in Christ is full and overflowing.

There are three distinct levels of supernatural abundance:

1. Just Enough: At this level, every child of God has what is needed for the moment. Needs are met, but there is no extra.

2. More Than Enough: Here, the believer not only meets present needs but also has surplus for the future. There is overflow and excess.

3. Inexhaustible Supply: This is the realm of trans-generational abundance. Like Abraham, your wealth and provision outlive you and bless generations to come. It is constant, supernatural supply, eternal and divine in nature.

God's will is for you to grow into the fullness of this abundance. So walk in faith, stewardship, and obedience because in Christ, you are destined for overflow.

Quote of the Day: The divine life we have received in Christ is full and overflowing.

PERSONAL RESPONSE:

1. Are you currently living at the level of "just enough," "more than enough," or "inexhaustible supply"? What may be limiting you from growing into the next level?
2. In what areas of your life do you need to trust God more deeply for supernatural provision?
3. How intentional are you in using your abundance, whether material or spiritual, for "every good work" that blesses others and glorifies God?

Daily Prayer: Father, I thank You for Your promise of supernatural abundance. I receive grace to walk in the fullness of Your provision, not just for my needs, but so I can abound in every good work and become a channel of blessing to others. Let my life overflow with divine supply, to the glory of Your name. Amen.

Read the Bible in One Year: Ecclesiastes 10-12; Galatians 1

AN INVITATION TO THE SUPERNATURAL REALM

"Come up hither and I will show you what must take place after now." Revelation 4:1

God is not limited by natural laws. He is supernatural by essence, and He created you in His image. That means you, too, are designed for supernatural living. But many believers confine their walk with God to the natural senses, never stepping into the realm of the extraordinary where God operates.

The supernatural is the domain where heaven and earth meet; where God reveals mysteries and works wonders beyond human logic. In Revelation 4:1, God called John to "come up higher," an invitation to operate from a higher realm. This same call is extended to every believer.

Elisha saw into the invisible realm (2 Kings 6), and his servant's eyes were opened to behold angelic armies. Jacob, in Genesis 28, saw a ladder connecting heaven and earth, confirming Bethel as the gate of heaven. Peter encountered the transfigured Christ on the mount (Luke 9), and Paul testified of being caught up to the third heaven (2 Corinthians 12).

These were not isolated events for special men; they are examples of what's available to you in Christ.

As we come to the end of this month and the end of this series of devotionals on the supernatural, God is calling you to rise beyond the limits of the natural. If you will walk with Him, you too can enter and operate from the supernatural realm, starting now.

Quote of the Day: God is not limited by natural laws. He is supernatural by essence, and He created you in His image. That means you, too, are designed for supernatural living.

PERSONAL RESPONSE:

1. Do you live with a daily awareness that you were created to operate beyond natural limitations?
2. What habits, thoughts, or fears are keeping you confined to a purely natural experience of God?
3. How can you intentionally respond to God's invitation to "come up higher" and live from the supernatural realm?

Daily Prayer: Heavenly Father, open my eyes to see beyond the natural. I receive grace to walk in constant fellowship with You and to dwell in the supernatural realm where Your power, presence, and wisdom flow freely. My Father God, lunch me into the new year with uncommon power, In Jesus' name, I pray. Amen.

Read the Bible in One Year: Song of Songs 1-3; Galatians 2

ABOUT JAMES O. NANJO

An amazing Top 120 best-selling author and facilitator of schoolofreshoil.org, Bishop James Nanjo is a personal development coach and spiritual growth mentor. He has visited over 45 nations for seminars, conferences, and missions. He has created resources that is making great difference through his online and in-person seminars, books, and the popular daily devotional "My Daily Solutions and Daily Restoration." Bishop Nanjo is the author of more than one hundred and twenty books and several online home study courses, transforming thousands of students around the world. He has ministered to over 60,000 people in a single service. His TV and radio program, "My Daily Solutions," is a weekly show of spiritual growth and personal development that has impacted many people. He is one of the leading voices in world missions with an emphasis on the Asia Pacific region, which has a population of over 4.5 billion people. He is a consecrated bishop, presiding over several churches around the world and serving as the lead pastor of Restoration City Church, a dynamic, multicultural, and apostolic ministry in London, UK, where he resides with his wife, Antonina, and their children. God is blessing and growing the global missions-centred ministry of Bishop James Nanjo through the BJ Nanjo Ministries.

JOIN THE BJ NANJO MINISTRIES GLOBAL FAMILY TODAY, BY SCANING THE QR CODE FOR ACCESS OR VISITING:
www.mydailysolutions.org/jamesnanjo

PARTNER WITH US TODAY

MY DAILY SOLUTIONS GLOBAL PARTNERS (MDSGP)

Our goal is to place this daily devotional in schools, universities, hospitals, homes, and all public places. Our target list includes nations, cities, towns, and even villages. Just imagine what will happen to the glory of God when you partner with us every month as MDSGP, to support our mandate of reaching multitudes with My Daily Solutions.

Below are ways you can become an MDSGP:

- You can partner with us to sponsor 50 copies or more, every quarter.
- You or your business can partner with us to adopt and sponsor a school, community, or city on monthly basis.
- You can partner with us by becoming a quarterly distributor of the devotional or you can become our covenant partner with a commitment of monthly donations that will help us communicate the good news of Jesus Christ in a city near you via TV, Radio, and Online.
- Your donation will also help our community initiative projects of building boreholes, helping orphans, and making donations to underprivileged communities.

Be a part of this special mission through your financial partnership with us to reach out and sponsor people in every city with the My Daily Solution message of Jesus Christ.

ACCOUNTS DETAILS

UK: WISE BANK: Sort Code: 231470 // Accounts Number: 91738664

GHANA: STANBIC BANK// Accounts Holder: James Nanjo// Accounts Number: 9040004417695

GHANA (MTN MOBILE MONEY): 0556729900

CASH APP: $JamesNanjo

PAYPAL: paypal.me/rccglobal

ZELLE: drnanjo@gmail.com

GET A COPY OF THE DAILY SOLUTIONS JOURNAL

MY DAILY SOLUTIONS JOURNAL

Get your copy today from Amazon.co.uk. This journal is a great resource for anyone interested in using My Daily Solutions for spiritual growth and spiritual progression. The 128 page journal will help you save wealth of golden information that will be useful for spiritual growth and in the future. You will stay committed to your daily devotional because of this journal.

Pages: 128 // ISBN: 9781907671852

GET YOUR COPIES OF THESE BOOKS AT:
WWW.MYDAILYSOLUTIONS.ORG

Printed in Dunstable, United Kingdom

67156873R00100